Foreword

Food, glorious food...how many of us have incredible memories of our families eating together? Whether they were notable meals or simple comfort food, eating together has long been a time-honored family tradition. This cookbook is about those family traditions, as seen through the experiences of one amazing family. The Fitzsimmons-Lepeska's have as many memories as the rest of us and when their health changed, they learned to make new memories around food.

This book is a tribute to creativity and a love of food. Ellen learned she was gluten-intolerant and dairy-intolerant—a tough mix for someone from Wisconsin. Middle-child Molly was diagnosed with type 1 diabetes in her early twenties. What to do? Quit eating? I don't think so. What they did is in these pages. They put their family heads together and came up with a delicious, inviting way to continue to eat as a family without giving up taste or those divine foods that you dream about.

As more and more people have eating challenges, how delightful it is to have Ellen put this together. Not only is it a quintessential piece on how to eat well with issues, it is a testament to family resiliency. With many families spending less time together, we can all use this prescription to achieve tasty innovative foods at family meals. Research indicates that families who eat together are more resilient to a variety of societal challenges. Now there are no excuses for not getting your family together and enjoying healthy family meals.

Hurrah for Ellen and her family, and here's to what they have brought you to try together. As a nutritionist, I love eating with her family and sharing what I learn there with mine. I encourage you to do the same. Food, glorious food...

Robin A. Orr, PhD
Adjunct Professor, Food Science & Human Nutrition
University of Illinois Urbana Champaign
Past President, Society for Nutrition Education

Contents

7 Meet Our Intolerant Family

13 Starters and Party Snacks
Tapenade ONE
Tapenade TWO
Spicy Roasted Red Pepper Dip
Gregg's Salsa
Emergency Salsa
Mango or Peach Cucumber Salsa ONE
Mango or Peach Salsa TWO
Tomatillo Guacamole
Guacamole
Toasted Nuts
Antipasto
Antipasto Dressing
Hummus
Spring Rolls with Vegetable Filling
Peanut Sauce
Spring Rolls Shrimp Filling
Spring Rolls Sauce

27 Soups
Carrot Curry Soup
Pear and Leek Soup
Roasted Veggie Soup
Chunky Red Chili
Green Tomatillo Chili
Seafood Tomato Soup
Thai Coconut Noodle Soup
Basic Vegetable Soup Plus
Basic Vegetable Beef
Southwestern Soup with Tortilla Chips
Seafood Chowder
Soup Stock

41 Salads
Basic Vinaigrette Dressing
Taco Salad
Chef's Salad
Curried Shrimp and Quinoa or Spinach Salad
 • Spinach and Shrimp Salad
 • Citrus Dressing
 • Quinoa and Shrimp Salad
 • Cucumber Dressing
Curried Chicken or Turkey Salad
Roasted Potato Salad
Wild Rice and Turkey or Chicken Salad
 • Wild Rice Dressing
Carrot Walnut Salad

The Intolerant Family Cookbook
Gluten-Free, Dairy-Free, Family Friendly Food

Ellen Fitzsimmons & Molly Lepeska

The Intolerant Family Cookbook
Gluten-Free, Dairy-Free, Family Friendly Food
by Ellen Fitzsimmons and Molly Lepeska

Copyright ©2009 by Ellen Fitzsimmons and Molly Lepeska
All rights reserved. Reproduction in whole or in part of any portion or in any form without permission of the author is prohibited.
Printing by Brioprint.com.

Individual and bulk orders of *The Intolerant Family Cookbook* are available at www.ifcookbook.com. For more information, contact ifcookbook@charter.net.

ISBN: 978-0-615-29087-4
Library of Congress Control Number: 2009932996

Editing: Mary Maher
Design: Zucker Design
Artwork: Johanne Grinde
Cover Photos: Christy Lafferty of Legacy Portraiture, www.PictureALegacy.com
With special appreciation for the many contributions of Heather Lepeska.

The recipes were analyzed by The Food Processor®SQL Version 10.00, ESHA Research, P.O. Box 13028, Salem OR 97309, for nutritional analysis. The analysis for each recipe refers to a single serving. Every effort was made to be accurate but the figures are intended for a guide only.

Orange Carrot Salad
Carrot Salad with Lime and Cilantro
Carrot and Pineapple Salad
Roasted Tomato and Grilled Red Pepper Salad
Asparagus with Tarragon Vinaigrette
Sweet and Sour Cucumbers with Dill
Ginger Cukes
Peanut Cole Slaw
Frizzled Leek Salad

59 Main Courses
Turkey Barbeque
Not Your Mother's Pot Roasted Chicken or Beef
Lemon Chicken with Ripe and Green Olives
Chicken Enchiladas with Salsa Verde
Chicken Pasta Dinner
Chicken Satay with Peanut Sauce
Turkey and Pear Sauté
Curried Beef
Beef Wrapped in Lettuce
Ground Turkey Wrapped in Lettuce
   • Sweet Chili Dipping Sauce
Hungarian Goulash
The Very Best Slow Oven Roasted Pork
Maple Chili Roasted Pork
Easy Kraut and Pork Chops
Tomato Curry Pork Chops
Apple Braised Pork Chops
Chicken and Broccoli
Easy Baked Fish
Sweet-Spicy Glazed Salmon
Super Fast Mediterranean Fish
When It Has to Be Fried Fish
Shrimp with Excellent Almond Pepper Sauce
Spinach Rice
Pesto Sauce for Fish or Chicken
Rice Noodle Bowl with Red Sauce
Ginger Rice Noodle Bowl

85 Veggies
Molly's Veggie Frittata
Ratatouille
Gourmet Veggie Pasta
Spinach Pesto for Pasta
Mashed Cauliflower
Fried Rice with Fruits and Vegetables
Roasted Asparagus
Red Cabbage
Faux Hash Browns
Oven Fries
Rosemary Baked Sweet Potatoes
Sort-of-Sweet Baked Sweet Potatoes

Sautéed Spinach
Grilled Corn on the Cob

97 Breads
Basic Bread
Brown Bread
Corn Bread
Good Flat Bread
Baked Polenta
Stirred Polenta
Josh's Polenta with Roasted Vegetables
Heather's Favorite German-Style Oven Pancake
Carrot Muffins
Gus' Blueberry Muffins

111 Desserts
Hazelnut Bars
Easy One-Bowl Brownies
Blonde Brownies
Lane's Bakery Nutty Crunchy Bars
Basic Chocolate Chip Cookies
Easy Sesame Almond Cookies
Peanut Butter Cookies
Mexican Wedding Cakes
Poppy Seed Cookies
Chocolate Pecan Cookies

Best Chocolate Pudding
Coconut Banana Custard
Strawberry or Raspberry Sorbet
Lemon Ice
Chocolate Nut Cake with Creamy Chocolate Frosting
Great Pumpkin Dessert
Angel Food Cake with Blueberry Sauce
Peach Crisp
Chocolate Nut Pie
Fudge
Chocolate Covered Hazelnuts
Peanut Butter Chocolate Candies

135 Good Food, Safe Food: Making it Work
Handy appliances
Shopping for GF/DF products
Emergency food pantry ideas
Intolerant entertaining

141 Recipe Index

144 IFC Tip Index

Meet Our Intolerant Family

Yes, we are an intolerant family but no, it is not because of the tattoos Molly came home with in high school or the fact Josh does not always cut his hair. We are a family that is intolerant to food. Intolerant to the food we love, the food we enjoyed nightly around the family table. Intolerant to many of the good things that represent the food-centered traditions we continue to enjoy as we come together from all over the world for a host of occasions.

Now we must monitor our food closely and find new ways to "feed" our shared enthusiasms. Because we are resilient, stubborn cooks, this intolerant family learned to turn a culinary challenge into an opportunity to rethink and expand our recipe repertoire. To paraphrase a popular saying, "when life gives you gluten intolerance you make gluten-free bread."

Our family spends some of its best times in the kitchen. We like all aspects of food preparation: planning meals, sharing recipes and shopping—especially at farmers markets. Most of all, we like crowding into the kitchen and getting in each other's way while preparing a family meal together.

Diet changes inspire cookbook

I was 50 years old when diagnosed with an intolerance to dairy products. Two years later, I added gluten intolerance to the list. At about the same time, Molly, then a senior in college, learned she had type 1 diabetes. It was a lot to deal with, especially for a family that loves food. Food intolerances or any health-enforced change in diet can turn a passion for food into a chore—if you let it.

That's why we wanted to write this book, using our family's experience to show that food can remain a fun and tasty family experience despite many challenges. We also appreciate that, while it is possible to have a good restaurant meal that meets dietary restrictions (and we still enjoy eating out), food intolerances make learning to prepare delicious food at home even more important.

The number of people with food intolerances is growing. We'll let medical science decide if this is due to an actual higher incidence or better diagnoses. Either way, there are now many children and young adults who find they must deal with food allergies, intolerances or lifelong health-enforced dietary changes.

This book focuses on food that is both gluten-free and dairy-free. We wanted to create a book with recipes that many people would enjoy. Nutritional content and carbohydrate counts are included for each recipe, which is of special importance for diabetics. Plus, we try to keep the fat and calorie counts reasonable without sacrificing taste.

People facing food intolerances for the first time quickly learn that eating at home is easier and safer than eating out. For those without much cooking experience, there is the added challenge of preparing food that meets very special dietary needs. None of the *Intolerant Family* recipes require a culinary background. But we encourage less-experienced cooks to start with the simpler recipes, of which there are many.

Most of all, we want this book to be a good choice for people with an intolerance of *bad tasting* food. We taste-tested all of the recipes in our own kitchens and served the results to family and friends. Our goal was to develop menu choices approved by food intolerant and food non-intolerant people alike. Most family members contributed recipes and those who don't cook became our brave designated taste testers.

Learning how to cook…all over again

Being a life-long cook doesn't prepare you for the challenges you face after developing food intolerances. You need to relearn and rethink the basics that once seemed simple. The days of saying "everything tastes better with enough butter and sugar" are over. But with patience and perseverance, you can learn how to be a great cook again with a new awareness of how to cook healthier. For novice cooks, adapting to a food intolerance means learning to be a healthy cook right from the start.

Preparing your kitchen

A gluten-free kitchen is a must for people who are gluten intolerant. For us, cross-contamination is a dreaded enemy. It is crucial to prevent kitchen cross-contamination by separating food preparation areas.

I eliminated all wheat flour or products containing gluten from the main cooking areas in my kitchen. Although I purchase bread for gluten-eating family members and guests, I no longer bake with wheat. Gluten eaters have their own toaster and one small counter in the kitchen where they handle all gluten-containing foods. Everywhere else is gluten-free. My toaster toasts only gluten-free food. All the remaining counter tops are gluten-free. The pantry contains no wheat flour and few products that contain gluten.

To the extent possible, I purchase gluten-free commercial products like mayonnaise and ketchup. If a gluten eater wants mayonnaise, they must use a clean spoon and spoon it from the jar to a dish. Ditto for peanut butter, marmalade or any other item shared by multiple family members. Another approach is to stock two of everything and make sure both have clear labels so the gluten frees never share with the gluten eaters.

Even before becoming food intolerant, I always was fussy about food safety and kitchen cleanliness. I used to tell the children to eat only what I brought to potlucks and did not condone children "dipping" into shared dishes at the dinner table. Now I am a zealot where food safety and the potential for cross-contamination is concerned.

Reading labels

In the summer of 2004, Congress passed the Food Allergen Labeling and Consumer Protection Act (P.L. 108-282). This act is an amendment to the Federal Food, Drug and Cosmetic Act, which governs the labeling of all foods, except meat products, poultry products and some egg products, regulated by the US Department of Agriculture. The 2004 legislation requires that all food containing any of eight common food allergens (milk, eggs, fish, crustaceans, tree nuts, wheat, peanuts and soybeans) spell this out in plain English on the label.

Manufacturers meet this requirement using one of two methods. The first method features a separate line after the ingredients list that says, for example, "This item contains wheat, almonds and milk." The other approved method is to include a parenthetical reference in the ingredient list, for example: "Ingredients: semolina (wheat), rice flour, rolled oats, pine nuts, tomato juice, whey (milk), sodium caseinate, and natural flavoring (peanuts)." Both cases show clear labeling of the allergen. The legislation set a deadline of January 1, 2006, for this labeling to occur. Note the rules do not require the food labels to disclose the presence of gluten itself. The same is true for rye and barley.

The Food Allergen Labeling and Consumer Protection Act also directed the Food and Drug Administration (FDA), an agency of the United States Department of Health and Human Services, to develop standards for certifying food as "gluten-free." This labeling of foods as gluten-free is voluntary, but all items with this label must meet the FDA standards now under development. Current information on the status of these standards is available at the Department of Health and Human Services website: www.cfsan.fda.gov/~dms/glutqa.html

The law does not cover all foods. Consumers must remain diligent about meat and poultry products and some egg products. A growing awareness of food-intolerance issues and potentially harmful ingredients is encouraging. There are grocery stores that carry sausages and meats—like pepperoni or certain hams—labeled gluten-free. And a number of manufacturers are doing a good job of putting information on their websites about the gluten content of their products.

Some processed meats contain milk products, but dairy- and gluten-free versions are available. The key is to review labels carefully, visit product websites for information or call the manufacturers. We find that freezing leftover roasts and grilled meats is an easy way to "create" our own sandwich or salad meats without worrying about ingredients added during processing.

People with newly diagnosed food intolerances or diabetes quickly learn never to eat anything commercially prepared without reading the label. In the old days, labels did not always disclose gluten-containing ingredients. The new labels are a tremendous help, but only if you read them. Get in the habit of reading the label before putting anything in your shopping cart because both milk and gluten show up in all kinds of unexpected places. For those with diabetes, the amount of sugar or other carbohydrates in a prepared food item can be staggering. Be especially wary of items labeled "lite." They often take out sugar but put other carbohydrates in, or add an assortment of additives.

We frequently have seen the international symbols for wheat-free, gluten-free and dairy-free on food items in Canada, where Josh lived, and in Amsterdam, where Molly lives now. Less evident in the US, these symbols are a wonderful assistance for food shoppers dealing with food intolerances.

The safest way to go is make fresh. It will taste better and probably be healthier, too.

Season to taste

A common complaint of both gluten-free and low-carb cooking is that the food is uninteresting or not tasty. The secret to zippy flavor is seasoning. And the best seasonings are fresh herbs and spices. Most grocery stores these days carry fresh herbs or you can grow your own, even if you live in a city apartment. If you lack a green thumb, there are excellent commercial sources for high-quality, dried gluten-free (GF) seasonings. We are fortunate to have a Penzey's store (local and online vendor for dried seasonings) within a mile of our home. Wherever you live, it is worth the time, effort and cost to use good-quality seasonings. But, as with other packaged foods, be diligent about reading the labels.

While doing the dietary analysis for this collection of recipes, we realized how easy it is to consume high levels of sodium. The recipes reproduced here use a minimum of commercially prepared products, but we do list ingredients like canned tomatoes or soup stock. Whenever possible, we use low-sodium or salt-free commercial versions of these and other products, and the dietary analysis reflects that. If you use products without one of those labels, expect a higher sodium count. A good rule of thumb is not to add additional salt during preparation when you prepare dishes that contain canned ingredients like stock or tomatoes. Taste the dish and if it needs more salt, start by adding a half-teaspoon of salt. Family and guests can add additional salt at the table according to taste. But everyone may find how easy it is to become accustomed to eating less salt.

Oils and shortening

In these recipes, we use no butter and very little hard shortening. Dairy-free, gluten-free margarine is available in some large grocery stores and in specialty stores. There also are products available that are free of transfats.

Stock your kitchen with at least two kinds of cooking oil. We typically use three: canola oil, a mild olive oil and an extra virgin olive oil. A good olive oil is always worth the splurge. Extra virgin olive oil is best for salad dressings. Canola oil has a higher smoking point than olive oil so is better for frying. Or you can combine canola and olive oils to create oil excellent for sautéing food. Whatever the oil, use the least amount possible to prepare your foods. Measure the oil you add to sauté food to ensure you do not add more than you think.

Fiber for health and good taste

There is growing appreciation for the importance of fiber in the diet, especially for diabetics. One good source of fiber is raw fruits and vegetables. For diabetics, bread made with whole-grain flour and high-fiber cereals also are an option.

We suggest trying gluten-free flour products that are higher in fiber for people with gluten intolerance alone or gluten intolerance and diabetes. There are a number of them now available. An easy way to improve the taste, texture and fiber content of your baked goods is to add two tablespoons of ground flax meal, sesame seeds or almond meal to all gluten-free bread products.

Abbreviations used in this book

Watch for these elements of editorial shorthand in the recipe pages—a few helpful references and visual reminders.

GF – Gluten-free

DF – Dairy-free

Indicates a "Faster Than Takeout" recipe that is quick and easy to prepare.

Indicates "Intolerant Family Cooks Tip" or additional information about a key ingredient or preparation method.

Starters & Party Snacks

When I first developed food intolerances, I was amazed to find how many foods made to serve with wine or cocktails contained dairy products or gluten. Frequently, I attended work functions that included a reception with wonderful appetizers that I surveyed with envy while eating my small plate of carrot sticks and broccoli, the only foods on the table I was certain were gluten-free and dairy-free.

It is a real challenge to eliminate sour cream, cream cheese and cheese in all forms here in Wisconsin, the Dairy State. At our house, wine and cheese is now wine and tapenade or wine and salsa. And since it is hard to find good tasting commercially prepared crackers that are gluten- and dairy-free, I often use raw vegetables to dip.

Many brands of corn chips, potato chips and some unflavored rice or soy chips also are gluten-free and dairy-free. Reserve those for the rare occasion when the urge for salty, low-nutritional value snacks is simply overwhelming. When friends invite you over for a cocktail party, they are surprised to learn the ubiquitous plain corn chip is a good snack-food choice.

MOLLY REMEMBERS: Heather and I used to love it when our parents hosted cocktail parties. One of our favorites was Mom's office Christmas party. We always felt so grown up helping to "cater" the event. Heather, who was shyer than I, would hold down the kitchen, refilling appetizer trays and decorating the desserts, while I acted as waitress, coat check, busboy and entertainment—if I could find anyone to listen to me, that is. Of course, the food was always delicious and homemade by Mom. Nothing fancy, but always great. I remember when I'd go to bed on these nights, I loved hearing the people still at the party talking and laughing. Before dropping off to sleep, I would think that maybe I had helped make people have such a good time. That joy in homespun entertaining is something important to my sister and me. It is a tradition we are happy to continue.

Tapenade ONE

1½ cup kalamata or other ripe olives, pitted
1 medium ripe tomato
10 large fresh basil leaves
2 garlic cloves
¼ cup extra virgin olive oil
2 T fresh lemon juice
2 t freshly ground black pepper
1 lb sliced carrot rounds or other fresh veggies for dipping

1. In food processor, pulse all ingredients until finely chopped. Do not puree.
2. Spoon tapenade into a shallow bowl and use as a dip for the carrots.

NUTRITIONAL STATS Servings 15, Serving size 39 g, Calories 100, Calories from fat 90, Total Fat 10 g, Saturated fat 1 g, Cholesterol 0 mg, Sodium 370 mg, Carbohydrates 3 g, Fiber 0 g, Protein 1 g

Tapenade TWO

This version uses grilled red peppers in place of half the ripe olives. It is less salty, a lower calorie tapenade with a milder taste.

¾ cup kalamata olives or other ripe olives, pitted
2 red peppers, grilled, skins removed, see page 16
10 large leaves fresh basil
2 garlic cloves
¼ cup extra virgin olive oil
2 t freshly ground pepper
1 lb sliced carrot rounds

1. Pulse all ingredients except carrots in a food processor. Do not puree.
2. Spoon tapenade into a shallow bowl and use as a dip for the carrots.

NUTRITIONAL STATS Servings 15, Serving size 32 g, Calories 60, Calories from fat 50, Total fat 6 g, Saturated fat .5 g, Cholesterol 0 mg, Sodium 90 mg, Carbohydrates 2 g, Fiber 0 g, Protein 0 g

ADD ONS & ALTERNATIVES Intolerants who tolerate goat cheese can top either tapenade version with goat cheese crumbles or a small log of goat cheese.

Roasting red peppers

Place red peppers quartered lengthwise and seeded on a baking sheet and place on a rack about one inch below the broiler in the oven. Char until black under broiler; this takes about 5 minutes. Remove from oven and place the peppers in a plastic bag, close tightly and let steam for 10 minutes. The skins will peel off easily.

Spicy Roasted Red Pepper Dip

Bottled red peppers are a good substitute for freshly roasted red peppers.

½ cup olive oil, divided
1 medium onion, thinly sliced
2 T ground cumin
1 t minced garlic
2 T minced jalapeno pepper
¼ cup molasses
6 roasted red peppers, skins removed
¼ cup fresh parsley, chopped
¼ cup lime juice
2 t salt
2 t black pepper

1. In a large sauté pan, heat one tablespoon of the olive oil over medium high heat until hot but not smoking.
2. Add the onion and cook, stirring occasionally, until translucent, five to seven minutes.
3. Add the cumin, garlic and jalapeno pepper and continue to cook, stirring frequently, for one minute.
4. Transfer the mixture to a food processor or blender and add the remaining ingredients.
5. Puree until very smooth. This mixture will last, covered and refrigerated, for several days.

Serve with carrots or other fresh veggies, GF crackers or corn chips. It is also a good spread to eat on sandwiches.

NUTRITIONAL STATS Servings 30, Serving size 40 g, Calories 50, Calories from fat 35, Fat 4 g, Saturated fat .5 g, Cholesterol 0 mg, Sodium 160 mg, Carbohydrate 4 g, Fiber 1 g, Protein 0

Gregg's Salsa

MOLLY RECALLS: During his college years, my husband Gregg worked at a terrific barbeque restaurant in Austin, Texas. He adapted this recipe from similar salsa served there. Although Gregg is funny, charming, diplomatic and good natured, I think it was probably this salsa that most endeared him to my parents. It has become a family favorite.

3 lbs canned unsalted whole tomatoes
3 lbs fresh tomatoes
2-3 jalapeno peppers
¼ cup olive oil
6-9 cloves of garlic, unpeeled
1-2 medium red onions, peeled and chopped
1 bunch fresh cilantro, washed and chopped
1 T cumin
2 limes, halved
2 t salt
2 t freshly ground white pepper

1. Preheat the oven to 400º.
2. Place the fresh tomatoes, peppers and garlic in a 9 x 13 baking dish and drizzle with the olive oil. Roast in the oven for 25 to 30 minutes.
3. Meanwhile, dice the onion, chop the cilantro, and drain the canned tomatoes.
4. When the tomato skins are lightly charred and flaky, remove the vegetables from the oven. Cool. Halve the tomatoes and remove the seeds. Remove any big pieces of tomato skin, leaving some charred bits. Cut the stems from the jalapeno peppers, remove the seeds and discard the skins from the garlic cloves.
5. In a blender, start layering the ingredients. Add a few cloves of garlic, one half to one jalapeno pepper, and layers of fresh tomatoes, onions, cilantro, cumin and canned tomatoes.
6. Repeat the layers until the top of the blender is reached. Add canned and fresh tomatoes in equal proportions. Add half a teaspoon salt, pepper and the juice from half a lime and pulse until the ingredients are mixed. Do not puree, the texture should be chunky.
7. Empty the blender contents into a large bowl. Taste the salsa and adjust the seasonings for the next two batches adding salt and pepper and the juice from half a lime to each batch. Six pounds of tomatoes should make three blenders full of salsa.
8. Serve warm or cold. This salsa keeps for up to a week in the refrigerator but it rarely goes uneaten that long.

NUTRITIONAL STATS Servings 35, Serving size 90 g, Calories 35, Calories from fat 15, Fat 1.5 g, Saturated fat 0, Cholesterol 0 mg, Sodium 140 mg, Carbohydrates 4 g, Fiber 1 g, Protein 1 g

More Salsas

Salsas are an excellent snack or appetizer that provide flavor, good nutrition and a little of the exotic to your bite-sized cuisine. Made from fruits and vegetables, salsas contain little fat or oil, and can have quite a zippy taste. Simple to prepare, salsas are an easy way to add nutrients and fiber to your daily diet while impressing your friends.

There is no single best way to make salsa so I encourage you to experiment. Make substitutions if you find yourself short of one ingredient. You might create a new flavor in the process. Just keep in mind: The secret to good salsa is texture and color, as well as taste. In our family, we like salsa spicy. But for those with more temperate palates, eliminate the hotter peppers and the pepper seeds to ensure a mellower blend of flavors. A hand blender makes all the chopping involved in salsa prep go really fast. The salsas featured here also work well as an accompaniment to meats like grilled chicken or pork tenderloin.

Emergency Salsa

This salsa is great for when unexpected company turns up or you get home late and hungry. Prepare it using ingredients available in your pantry and refrigerator. Not quite on a par with Gregg's Salsa, this "emergency" mix still tastes good.

1 14.5 oz can unsalted diced tomatoes, including juice
2 slices canned mango, well drained, rinsed and diced or
   1 fresh mango, diced
1 pepper, red, green, or yellow pepper, diced
1 medium red onion, diced
3 cloves garlic, minced
2 T parsley, chopped
2 T cilantro, chopped or 2 t dried cilantro
1 T olive oil
¼ cup red wine vinegar or lime juice
1 t salt
2 t freshly ground pepper
1-2 t cayenne or other hot pepper

1. Combine all ingredients.
2. Adjust salt, pepper and cayenne pepper if necessary.

NUTRITIONAL STATS Servings 15, Serving size 66 g, Calories 30, Calories from fat 10, Fat 1 g, Saturated fat 0 g, Cholesterol 0 mg, Sodium 170 mg, Carbohydrates 5 g, Fiber 1 g, Protein 1 g

STARTERS & PARTY SNACKS

Mango or Peach Cucumber Salsa ONE

1 ripe mango, peeled and diced or 2 ripe peaches, diced
1 cucumber, seeded, peeled and diced
1 medium onion, chopped fine
1 red, yellow or orange pepper, finely chopped
1 jalapeno pepper, finely chopped, seeds included
2 T fresh cilantro, finely chopped
1 T olive oil
1 T red wine vinegar
½ t salt
1 t freshly ground pepper

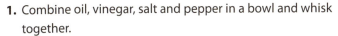

1. Combine oil, vinegar, salt and pepper in a bowl and whisk together.
2. Blend the onion, peppers and cilantro with a hand blender until very finely chopped, or chop by hand with a sharp knife.
3. Place the diced mango or peaches and cucumber in a bowl. Add the onion mixture and the vinegar and oil mixture and stir to blend.

NUTRITIONAL STATS Servings 15, Serving size 39 g, Calories 25, Calories from fat 10, Fat 1 g, Saturated fat 0 g, Cholesterol 0 mg, Sodium 80 mg, Carbohydrates 4 g, Fiber 1 g, Protein 0 g

Mango or Peach Salsa TWO

1 14.5-oz can unsalted diced tomatoes, drained
1 mango or 2 peaches, peeled and diced
1 medium onion, chopped fine
1 jalapeno pepper, seeded and minced
10 good-sized fresh basil leaves, chopped
1 T olive oil
1 T lime juice
½ t salt
1 t or more freshly ground pepper

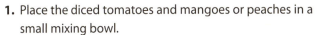

1. Place the diced tomatoes and mangoes or peaches in a small mixing bowl.
2. Mince the onion, pepper and basil with a hand blender or sharp knife.
3. Add the onion, pepper and basil mixture to the fruits
4. Add the olive oil, lime juice, salt and pepper, and mix until all are blended.

NUTRITIONAL STATS Servings 20, Serving size 49 g, Calories 25, Calories from fat 5, Fat 1 g, Saturated fat 0 g, Cholesterol 0 mg, Sodium 65 mg, Carbohydrates 4 g, Fiber 1 g, Protein 0 g

Tomatillo Guacamole

What is it about the avocado that makes it so good? We like just slicing one as a topping for a salad and all kinds of guacamole recipes. Since I no longer eat cheese, I often substitute guacamole as a topping for chili, tacos or enchiladas.

1 T olive oil
8 tomatillos,* husked, washed and cut in half
1 clove garlic, peeled and minced
2 T cilantro, chopped
½ small onion, chopped
1 T lime juice
1 avocado, peeled and pitted
½ t salt
1 t freshly ground pepper

* Meet the tomatillo on page 35.

1. Place the olive oil in a medium sauté pan over medium heat.
2. Add the onion, garlic and tomatillos, and sauté until tomatillos are light brown.
3. Remove from heat and let cool. When the tomatillo mixture is cool, combine with remaining ingredients and blend with a hand blender or food processor until well blended.
4. Serve with fresh veggies or corn chips.

NUTRITIONAL STATS Servings 15, Serving size 35 g, Calories 35, Calories from fat 25, Fat 3 g, Saturated fat 0 g, Cholesterol 0 mg, Sodium 80 mg, Carbohydrate 3 g, Dietary fiber 1 g, Protein 0 g

Guacamole

1 medium red onion, finely chopped
2 cloves of garlic, finely minced
1 ripe tomato, peeled and chopped
1 jalapeno pepper, finely chopped, seeds optional
1 t salt
2 t powdered cumin
2 T lime juice
3 avocados, pitted and peeled

1. Combine the finely chopped onion, garlic, tomato, jalapeno pepper, salt, cumin and lime juice.
2. Mash avocado in a bowl. Add the onion and tomato mixture and stir to combine ingredients.
3. Taste and add additional salt or lime juice if needed.

NUTRITIONAL STATS Servings 20, Serving size 46 g, Calories 50, Calories from fat 40, Fat 4.5 g, Saturated fat .5 g, Cholesterol 0 mg, Sodium 120 mg, Carbohydrate 4 g, Fiber 2 g, Protein 1 g

Toasted Nuts

1½ t onion powder
½ t garlic powder
1 t kosher salt (split)
1 t curry powder
¼ t cayenne pepper
2 T canola oil
2 T honey
3 cup raw pecan halves or other favorite nuts

1. Preheat oven to 250° F. Line large rimmed baking sheet with foil.
2. Mix onion powder, garlic powder, three-quarters teaspoon salt, curry powder and cayenne pepper in small bowl.
3. In a heavy medium saucepan over medium heat, melt the oil and honey with remaining salt. Add the spice mixture and stir to blend.
4. Add the nut halves and stir until well coated.
5. Remove from heat.
6. Spread nuts in single layer on the prepared baking sheet.
7. Bake the pecans until dry and toasted, about 40 minutes.
8. Cool completely and separate the pecans. The nuts will keep for a week in an airtight container at room temperature.

NUTRITIONAL STATS Servings 16, Serving size 26 g, Calories 170, Calories from fat 150, Fat 16 g, Saturated fat 1.5 g, Cholesterol 0 mg, Sodium 150 mg, Carbohydrate 5 g, Dietary fiber 2 g, Protein 2 g

Antipasto

Antipasto is one of those dishes that looks like it took hours to prepare but only takes minutes. The secret to an excellent antipasto tray is an attractive display, so include foods that add color, texture and interesting shape. Supplement the antipasto suggestions that follow with GF/DF pepperoni or salami, hard-cooked egg slices or a can of white tuna packed in olive oil to create a heartier tray.

1 lb asparagus, discard any woody portion of stalks
    or 1 lb green beans
5 roma tomatoes, cut into rounds, either fresh
    or roasted tomatoes work well
1 15 oz can artichoke bottoms, well drained, rinsed and
    cut in halves
1 14 oz can hearts of palm, well drained, rinsed and cut in
    2 inch segments
1 red and 1 yellow pepper, grilled and skin removed,
    cut in strips
½ cup ripe and green olives
10 or 15 lettuce leaves

1. Steam asparagus or green beans about three minutes, vegetables should be crisp.
2. Drain asparagus or beans; cool immediately in ice water.
3. Place the vegetables, except for the asparagus or beans, in a large flat refrigerator container.
4. Pour half of the dressing over the vegetables, cover and marinate for 2 hours or overnight.
5. Place lettuce leaves on a serving platter and arrange the vegetables, including the asparagus or green beans, on the lettuce leaves. Drizzle the remaining dressing over all.

NUTRITIONAL STATS Servings 12, Serving size 173 g, Calories 140, Calories from fat 90, Fat 10 g, Saturated fat 1.5 g, Cholesterol 0 mg, Sodium 510 mg, Carbohydrate 11 g, Fiber 4 g, Protein 4 g

Antipasto dressing

3 T white wine vinegar
1 clove garlic, minced
½ t salt
1 t GF mustard
2 t freshly ground pepper
2 t oregano
2 t dried basil or 1 T fresh chopped
2 t marjoram
2 t sugar
½ cup olive oil

1. Combine all ingredients but the oil and blend.
2. Whisk the oil into the vinegar mixture and continue mixing until well blended.

NOTE: Nutritional stats for the antipasto include the dressing.

Hummus

Hummus is a great way to add fiber to your diet. You can find good GF/DF hummus in large grocery stores and specialty markets. However, it is quick and easy to make your own using canned garbanzo beans. It makes a handy last-minute snack for unexpected friends and a good sandwich spread.

1 large clove garlic, peeled
1 shallot, peeled and chopped
Juice of two limes and zest
½ cup water
⅓ cup olive oil, reserving 1 T
¼ cup parsley leaves, a few additional leaves for garnish
¼ cup mint leaves, a few additional leaves for garnish
1 15 oz can garbanzo beans, drained
1 t cumin
½ cup tahini
1 t salt
1 t pepper
2 T pine nuts or slivered almonds, toasted
Carrot rounds or GF crackers for dipping

1. Place the garlic, shallot, lime juice, zest, water and all but one tablespoon of the olive oil into a food processor. Blend until garlic and shallot are minced.
2. Add the remaining ingredients and pulse until pureed to a creamy consistency. If necessary, add additional water a tablespoon at a time.
3. Spread the hummus on a plate, drizzle the remaining olive oil over the top, and sprinkle with nuts and reserved parsley or mint leaves.

NUTRITIONAL STATS Servings 20, Serving size 50 g, Calories 100, Calories from fat 70, Fat 8 g, Saturated fat 1 g, Cholesterol 0 mg, Sodium 200 mg, Carbohydrate 6 g, Fiber 2 g, Protein 3 g

Spring Rolls

A neighbor introduced me to making my own spring rolls. Being crust-phobic, I anticipated a difficult time making a roll that looked attractive. But I was pleasantly surprised at how easy the skins are to work with and how quickly the rolls come together. Asian food stores and grocery stores with large Asian foods sections sell spring roll skins that are inexpensive and keep well. Both tapioca and rice skins are suitable for a GF diet and work with this recipe. A rice and tapioca combination skin is available now and easy to handle.

    Spring rolls are another food that allows you to let your imagination run wild with creative options for fillings. I offer two options for sauce and two options for fillings, and encourage you to experiment. After successfully preparing my first solo batch, I excitedly shared the news with Molly, who said: "Oh sure, I've been making those for years."

Spring Rolls with Vegetable Filling

8 spring roll skins—can be rice or tapioca, dinner-plate size
8 leaves of leafy lettuce such as Boston bibb or leafy red lettuce, spines removed and torn into 3-to-4 inch sections
1 cup additional lettuce, roughly chopped
1 cucumber, peeled and very thinly sliced
16 leaves each of basil, mint, fennel, cilantro or other favorite herbs
4 spring onions cut in 3-inch long slivers, white and light green parts
1 oz rice noodles, the thinnest size, sometimes called rice sticks
1 cup shredded carrots

NUTRITIONAL STATS Servings 8, Serving size 46 g, Calories 35, Calories from fat 0, Fat 0 g, Saturated fat 0 g, Cholesterol 0 mg, Sodium 20 mg, Carbohydrate 8 g, Fiber 1 g, Protein 1 g

Peanut Sauce

½ cup peanut butter
1 T mild molasses
1 T plum or black raspberry jam
1 T fish sauce
1 t hot pepper such as cayenne
1 lime, juiced
1 T finely minced pepper, jalapeno or green
1 T minced shallot or onion

1. Combine all the ingredients for the sauce and stir until well blended. If the sauce is too thick, add additional warm water, one tablespoon at a time.
2. To assemble the rolls, set up the vegetables in individual small bowls in assembly line fashion.
3. Place a large frying pan on the stovetop and place about one inch of water in the pan. Keep the water in the pan warm, but cool enough that you can always put your hand in the water.
4. Put one tapioca or rice skin in the water to soften. This takes 20 to 30 seconds. The skin should be pliable when ready to use.
5. Take out the skin and set it on a flat surface such as a large cutting board.
6. Place a lettuce section in the bottom third center of the tapioca skin. Stack more torn lettuce, the veggies and rice sticks on top of the lettuce.
7. Spread half a tablespoon of sauce over the veggies.
8. Carefully roll the skin from the bottom to the center, and then fold in the sides as you continue to roll.
9. Place the completed roll seam side down on a clean plate.
10. Continue assembling the rolls one at time. Serve with additional dipping sauce, if desired.

NUTRITIONAL STATS Servings 16, Serving size 33g, Calories 110, Calories from fat 70, Fat 8 g, Saturated fat 1 g, Cholesterol 0 g, Sodium 250 mg, Carbohydrate 6 g, Fiber 1 g, Protein 4 g

Spring Rolls Filling TWO – Shrimp

Try this shrimp filling for a more substantial spring roll. Or substitute the beef or minced turkey fillings for lettuce wraps found in the *Main Courses* section.

1 T oil
1 small sliced onion
2 cup grated cabbage
1 cup raw peeled and deveined shrimp

1. Heat the oil in a frying pan over medium heat and add the onion and cabbage. Cook for three minutes.
2. Add the shrimp and cook stirring occasionally for five minutes or until shrimp is pink and cooked through.
3. Remove from heat and roughly chop the shrimp.
4. Follow the directions for the spring rolls, placing about one tablespoon of shrimp filling on top of the vegetables before rolling up the rolls.

NUTRITIONAL STATS Servings 8 Serving size 136 g Calories 80 Calories from fat 20 Fat 2.5 g Saturated fat 0 g Cholesterol 45 mg Sodium 60 mg Carbohydrate 8 g Fiber 2g Protein 7 g

Spring Rolls Sauce TWO

For people like my husband, who do not like peanut butter, this spring roll sauce uses GF ketchup. Make it less spicy by eliminating the jalapeno.

½ cup GF ketchup
¼ cup cider vinegar
2 T molasses
2 T fish sauce
½ minced jalapeno pepper
1 minced shallot or small onion

1. Combine ingredients and use ½ T for each spring roll and the rest as a dipping sauce.

NUTRITIONAL STATS Servings 8, Serving size 43 g, Calories 35, Calories from fat 0, Fat 0 g, Saturated fat 0 g, Cholesterol 0 mg, Sodium 540 mg, Carbohydrate 9 g, Fiber 0 g, Protein 0 g

Soups

When you live in Wisconsin, a place where rosy-cheeked autumn turns suddenly into face-freezing winter, soup season is vital. For those winter days that chill us to the bone, we call out the big guns—spicy, heavy soups and chili. Most of the soups featured here are substantial enough to anchor the meal. The section leads off with recipes for two soups that make a great first course or, paired with a heavy salad, become a complete meal.

When recipes call for soup stock, consider making turkey stock and freezing it in small containers. This ensures the stock contains no gluten and is low in salt. If you prefer ready-made stock, GF chicken, beef and vegetable stock is available commercially. But since stock is often high in sodium, look for the brands that offer reduced sodium.

There are two different schools of thought in our family on soup consistency: the pro-chunky soupers and the pro-puree soupers. If you gravitate to the puree side, consider purchasing a hand blender. Hand blenders are safer and easier to use than a food processor for blending batches of hot soup. Although the first three soups in this section make a good pureed soup, you also can enjoy them in a chunkier state.

Now a warning. My family of enthusiastic cooks and taste testers believe you can (almost) never have a soup that is too spicy or has too much curry in it. If your taste runs to the slightly less spirited, lighten up on the spices.

Carrot Curry Soup

This is a soup that people who do not like cooked carrots really like. Thanks to the main ingredient, the soup is a great source of vitamin A, which every mother will tell you is essential for seeing in the dark and when up late on weekend nights waiting for teenagers to come home. Add additional water if the consistency is too thick.

1 cup chopped onions
1 clove garlic, minced
2 T olive oil
½ cup chopped celery
1 pound carrots, cleaned and peeled
1 T fresh ginger, minced, or 1 t powdered ginger
2 t curry powder
1 t hot pepper flakes or cayenne pepper, less for a milder soup
3 cups GF low-sodium stock or water
3 T natural peanut butter
½ cup coconut milk, optional
Salted peanuts for garnish, optional

1. In a large saucepan or Dutch oven over medium heat, sauté the onions and garlic in the olive oil until soft and mushy.
2. Add the carrots and celery. Sauté for 3 or 4 minutes.
3. Add the spices and the stock. Cover the soup and simmer for 20 minutes or until carrots are soft.
4. Add the peanut butter and coconut milk if used and puree the entire soup until smooth. Serve with salted peanuts sprinkled on top.

NUTRITIONAL STATS Servings 6, Serving size 289 g, Calories 200, Calories from fat 120, Fat 14 g, Saturated fat 5 g, Cholesterol 15 mg, Sodium 160 mg, Carbohydrate 1 g, Fiber 4 g, Protein 6 g

Picking a peanut butter

In recipes that call for peanut butter, we always use "natural" non-hydrogenated peanut butter. Look for products with only peanuts and possibly salt as ingredients. Some peanut butters have additives that add nothing you want in what you are cooking. You can find natural peanut butter on the shelf with other peanut butters in any grocery store. It does not need to be organic or fresh ground. Non-hydrogenated peanut butter separates at room temperature and oil rises to the top of the jar. Eliminate this problem by stirring it after you bring it home from the store and refrigerating.

Pear and Leek Soup

Consider this light, almost-sweet soup as a first-course complement to a pork roast or a flavorful summer soup. The potato serves as a thickening agent.

2 big leeks, well cleaned, sliced crosswise, use white part only
¼ cup olive oil
3 cups low-sodium GF broth
3 pears, peeled and cored, cut in chunks
1 small potato, peeled and diced
1 lime
¾ cup dry white wine
½ t salt
1 t pepper

1. In a large saucepan or Dutch oven, sauté the sliced leeks in the olive oil until tender.
2. Add the broth, pears and potato, and simmer for 30 minutes.
3. Add the wine, the juice of the lime, the salt and pepper, and simmer for 10 minutes more.
4. Puree before serving.

NUTRITIONAL STATS Servings 6, Serving size 267 g, Calories 190, Calories from fat 90, Fat 10 g, Saturated fat 1.5 g, Cholesterol 0 mg, Sodium 230 mg, Fiber 3 g, Protein 3 g

Cleaning leeks

Leeks can look clean on the outside but still be surprisingly dirty inside. To clean a leek, slice it in half vertically and gently pull the layers apart under running cold water. This washes away the grit that often collects between the layers. Use only the white and light green parts of the leek.

Roasted Veggie Soup

This recipe comes from a good friend of ours who likes garlic. If you are not a big fan of garlic, simply reduce the garlic or replace it with shallots.

2½ cups onion, roughly chopped
5 plum or Roma tomatoes, halved
6 large garlic cloves
1 cup carrots, chopped
1 cup potatoes, cubed
2 T olive oil
1 t salt
1 t pepper
4 cups low-sodium GF broth
1 t oregano
1 t basil
1 28-oz can diced unsalted tomatoes

1. Preheat the oven to 425°. Place the onion, fresh tomatoes, potatoes and carrots in a large roasting pan. Drizzle olive oil over the vegetables and sprinkle with salt and pepper.
2. Place the garlic cloves together at one end of the pan. Put the pan on the top rack of the oven.
3. Check the vegetables after 10 minutes and remove the garlic when it is light brown. Remove skins from the garlic
4. Roast the remaining vegetables for an additional 20 minutes, or until they are tender and lightly browned.
5. Combine the GF broth, oregano, basil and the canned tomatoes with their juice in a Dutch oven. Bring to boil; reduce heat and simmer for 15 minutes.
6. Add the roasted vegetables. Puree the soup mixture using a hand blender or puree in a food processor in batches. Add additional water if the soup is too thick.

NUTRITIONAL STATS Servings 10, Servings size 280 g, Calories 100, Calories from fat 30, Fat 3.5 g, Saturated fat .5 g, Cholesterol 0 mg, Sodium 300 mg, Carbohydrate 14 g, Fiber 2 g, Protein 4 g

Cooking with canned tomatoes

Watch out for canned tomatoes that are pre-seasoned because they may be loaded with salt. Use products that list the fewest *additional* ingredients to avoid unexpected taste surprises. If the only canned tomatoes available have salt, eliminate or reduce the amount of salt you use in recipes. Add more to taste before serving or at the table.

Chili: A Family Tradition

Chili is a family tradition and winter-party favorite at our house. I often prepared a big pot of it on Saturdays so that the family and assorted friends who were around could grab a bowl whenever they felt like it. Chili also is great for entertaining. I bought a big stack of inexpensive ceramic bowls to use for fun and easy winter chili parties. Once they have their steaming bowl of chili, guests help themselves to a variety of toppings—like veggies, chips, cheeses and salsa. Our tried-and-true family favorites are Chunky Red Chili and Green Tomatillo Chili.

Chunky Red Chili

This recipe makes eight servings but you can double, triple or quadruple it if you like. Use a stockpot or Dutch oven to prepare.

2 T canola oil
1 cup chopped onion
1 cup chopped peppers, green, red, yellow or a combination
2 cloves garlic, chopped
2 lbs beef stew meat
1 28-oz can diced unsalted tomatoes
¼ to ⅓ cup chili powder
¾ cup hearty red wine, optional
2 or more cups water
1 t salt
2 t black pepper

Add additional hot pepper (like cayenne) or a couple of dried red chilies to the soup if you prefer it hot.

Chili toppings—provide a selection
½ cup chopped tomatoes
2 cups GF/DF corn chips
½ cup chopped peppers
¾ cup shredded cheese

1 cup guacamole or 2 avocados, peeled, pitted and sliced

1 cup shredded lettuce

1. In a Dutch oven over medium high heat, sauté the onion, garlic and peppers in oil until vegetables are soft.
2. Add beef and cook until browned.
3. Add the tomatoes and juice, chili powder, salt and pepper, the wine (if used) and water.
4. Simmer for 2 hours or until meat is soft on top of the stove, or place in the oven at 350°. When the meat is tender, reduce the temperature to warm until time to serve. Add additional water as needed.
5. Serve with cheese (for the dairy tolerant), tomatoes, avocado, lettuce, peppers, GF corn chips or other favorite toppings.

NUTRITIONAL STATS Servings 8, Serving size 296 g, Calories 250, Calories from fat 100, Fat 11 g, Saturated fat 3 g, Cholesterol 70mg, Sodium 380 mg, Carbohydrate 7 g, Fiber 1 g, Protein 23 g

Note: Nutritional stats do not include toppings.

ADD ONS & ALTERNATIVES Prepare a *vegetarian* Chunky Red Chili by replacing the beef with two cups pinto beans, soaked overnight or simmered on the stove for three hours. We also like to add a few additional dried red hot peppers to this version. When entertaining with chili, we often make both versions. Many of our guests like to mix the two for a delicious chili combination. Another option is to add beans to the beef chili as you prepare it. For some reason, we always keep them separate.

Molly Recalls: The best part about these chili recipes for me is they allow for some creativity and, in turn, are quite forgiving. When Heather and I lived together in Washington, DC, right after I graduated from college, we threw a chili house-warming party. We made both the red and the tomatillo chilis, but decided to make chicken instead of beef tomatillo chili because we had a lot of non-red meat eating friends. For some reason, at the last minute, we decided the amount of chicken in our chili was inadequate and decided to throw in a bar of tofu. Surprisingly, the chili was still a big hit.

Green Tomatillo Chili

Were I to choose my favorite dish in this collection, it probably would be Green Tomatillo Chili. Whenever I make it, I get requests to make it again. I serve this chili at informal parties and take it to potlucks. Over the years, I prepared it for my children's teen and college friends, and future spouses. This version makes enough for a crowd. Fair warning: leftovers disappear unless well hidden.

This recipe calls for fresh tomatillos. If these are not available, use the equivalent amount of canned tomatillos—not quite as tasty but sometimes more convenient. Although this chili is full of flavor, it is not spicy hot so it is a good choice when serving guests who prefer milder food.

½ cup canola oil
2 large chopped onions, white onions are best
2 large cloves of garlic, peeled and sliced
1-2 cups chopped green pepper
4 lbs beef stew meat
2 bunches fresh cilantro, well washed
2 bunches fresh parsley
4-5 lbs fresh tomatillos, husked, washed and halved
2 cups low-sodium GF stock
2 cups water
1 t salt
1 t ground pepper
2 t ground cumin
2 t ground Mexican oregano
¼ cup corn meal mixed into ¾ cup water, optional

Chili toppings—provide a selection
1 cup chopped tomatoes
1 cup chopped peppers
1 cup chopped onions
3 cups GF corn chips
2 cups guacamole or sliced avocados
1 cup salsa, commercial or freshly made

1. Sauté onions, garlic and green pepper in the canola oil over medium high heat in a Dutch oven or stockpot until the vegetables are soft.
2. Add the beef and brown.
3. Chop the cilantro, parsley and tomatillos in food processor or blender in batches and add to the meat.
4. Stir in the stock and 2 cups of water.
5. Add the salt, pepper, cumin and oregano, stir and simmer for at least 3 hours. Add additional water as necessary.
6. For a thicker soup, mix the cornmeal with water to make 1 full cup. About 30 minutes before serving, raise the heat until the soup is bubbly and add the cornmeal mixture, stirring constantly. Simmer for 10 more minutes until soup thickens.

Spoon into bowls and let guests add their favorite toppings. You can make this chili a day ahead and reheat. Like other soups, often it is even better the next day.

NUTRITIONAL STATS Servings 18, Serving size 261 g, Calories 260, Calories from fat 130, Fat 15 g, Saturated fat 3.5 g, Cholesterol 65 mg, Sodium 180 mg, Carbohydrate 11 g, Fiber 3 g, Protein 21g

Note: Nutritional stats do not include toppings.

Meet the tomatillo

The tomatillo is a small, round pale-green or yellow fruit about the size and shape of a cherry tomato. It has a light brown husk that peels off easily, sometimes leaving a sticky residue that washes off. Look for tomatillos in the fresh fruit and vegetable sections of large grocery stores, most often near the tomatoes. Other sources are the grocery's Mexican food section or Mexican grocery stores.

Coconut milk: a little goes a long way

Thanks to its high fat and sugar content, coconut milk adds a creamy touch to recipes. Fortunately, it takes only a small quantity of this rich ingredient to give soups a creamy consistency and satisfy a craving for a cream-based soup. Coconut milk also is delicious in desserts. Most recipes do not need an entire can, so freeze the leftover in half-cup containers for use at a later time.

Seafood Tomato Soup

After having a soup similar to this in a restaurant with a GF menu, I went home and tried to duplicate it. My effort is not an exact match, but still very good. Omit the seafood for a good cream of tomato soup. Coconut milk provides rich, creamy texture and flavor.

1 large red onion, chopped
2 shallots, chopped or 2 cloves of garlic, chopped
1 T olive oil
1 small potato, diced and peeled
1 28-oz. can unsalted diced tomatoes, including juice
1 T curry powder
1 cup water
½ cup coconut milk
½ lb of scallops
¾ lb peeled and deveined shrimp
½ t salt
1 t pepper

1. In a large saucepan over medium-high heat, sauté the onions and shallots in the oil until soft.
2. Add the curry powder, potato, water and tomatoes, and simmer about 20 minutes.
3. Puree with a hand blender when the potatoes are soft.
4. Add the fresh seafood and heat through, about 5 minutes. The shrimp will be pink.
5. Stir in coconut milk, salt and pepper, and heat until hot.

NUTRITIONAL STATS Servings 6, Serving size 355 g, Calories 220, Calories from fat 70, Fat 8 g, Saturated fat 4 g, Cholesterol 100 mg, Sodium 400 mg, Carbohydrate 19 g, Fiber 4 g, Protein 21 g

Thai Coconut Noodle Soup

Molly Suggests: I make mine with thin rice noodles. Leave out the noodles to further reduce the carbs and make it more of a first course soup.

2 T canola oil
2 cloves garlic, chopped
1 lb chicken breasts cut into thin strips
2 T minced ginger
1 12-oz can coconut milk
2 cups GF, low-sodium soup stock or water
1 red pepper, cored, seeded and chopped
½ medium red onion, chopped
5 new potatoes, cut in fourths, cooked halfway through
4 green onions, chopped, save green tops
½ hot chile, chopped
2 T fish sauce
2 oz thin rice noodles, about ⅓ of a package
3 green onion tops for garnish
2 T chopped peanuts for garnish

1. Put the oil in a Dutch oven over medium-high heat and add the garlic, ginger and chicken.
2. Sauté until the chicken is light brown.
3. Add the coconut milk, soup stock, vegetables, seasonings and the fish sauce.
4. Bring to a boil, then simmer for 8 to 10 minutes.
5. Meanwhile, prepare the rice noodles according to package directions, usually soaking noodles in warm water for about 10 minutes.
6. Drain the noodles and use kitchen shears to cut the noodles in half or quarter pieces.
7. Combine the noodles with the soup; serve immediately.
8. Garnish with green onions and peanuts.

NUTRITIONAL STATS Servings 6, Serving size 365 g, Calories 440, Calories from fat 180, Fat 21 g, Saturated fat 12 g, Cholesterol 40 mg, Sodium 540 mg, Carbohydrate 42 g, Fiber 4 g, Protein 23 g

What is fish sauce?

Fish sauce is fermented fish. As gross as that sounds, it is a delicious, inexpensive substitute for wheat-laden soy sauce. Fish sauce is strongly flavored and high in sodium, so do not overuse. Eliminate salt in recipes that use fish sauce. A common ingredient in Asian cooking, look for it in Asian food stores or the Asian food section of large grocery stores. Rice Bowl with Red Sauce in the Main Course chapter feautures fish sauce. When Heather prepared it for her new husband—a man who eats anything—he took one whiff and backed away. Once she coaxed him to try it, he ate three servings. Assure guests that food made with this ingredient tastes better than it smells

Basic Vegetable Soup Plus

This basic soup provides a base for three very different tasting soups. If you like beans, add a can of garbanzo or pinto beans to any of these recipes or as a substitute for the meat and a great boost of fiber. Preparing the soups in a large soup pot or Dutch oven makes clean up easy.

1. In a Dutch oven over medium-high heat, brown the ground beef with the onions, shallots, garlic and celery.
2. Add the remaining ingredients, cover and simmer until the vegetables are soft, about 20 minutes.

NUTRITIONAL STATS Servings 6, Serving size 404 g, Calories 220, Calories from fat 30, Fat 3 g, Saturated fat 1 g, Cholesterol 40 mg, Sodium 120 mg, Carbohydrate 30 g, Fiber 4 g, Protein 18 g

Basic Vegetable or Basic Vegetable Beef ONE

For vegetable soup, omit the beef and add 1 T canola oil.

1 lb lean ground beef
1 medium onion, chopped
1 shallot or 1 clove of garlic, chopped
½ cup celery, chopped
2 large potatoes, cubed
1 cup cubed carrots
2 T chopped fresh parsley
1 28-oz can unsalted diced tomatoes
1 cup water
½ t salt
1 t black pepper

Southwestern Soup with Tortilla Chips TWO

2 T canola oil
2 boneless, skinless chicken breasts cut in ½-inch wide strips
1 medium onion, chopped
1 shallot, chopped
½ cup chopped celery
2 T chopped cilantro
1 t cumin
2 t chili powder
1 t pepper
½ t salt
2 large potatoes, cubed
1 cup cubed carrots
1 28-oz can unsalted diced tomatoes
1 cup water

1. Put the oil in a Dutch oven over medium-high heat. Add the chicken, onions and celery, and sauté until the chicken is lightly browned and the vegetables are soft.
2. Add the cilantro, cumin, chili powder, pepper and salt to the chicken and stir to combine.
3. Add the potatoes, carrots, tomatoes and water and simmer until the potatoes and carrots are soft.
4. Serve with GF corn chips.

NUTRITIONAL STATS Servings 6, Serving size 361 g, Calories 230, Calories from fat 50, Fat 6 g, Saturated fat .5 g, Cholesterol 25 mg, Sodium 90 mg, Carbohydrate 31 g, Fiber 4 g, Protein 13 g

Note: Nutritional stats do not include corn chips.

Seafood Chowder THREE

FASTER THAN TAKE-OUT

2 T canola oil
1 medium onion, chopped
1 shallot, chopped
½ cup chopped celery
2 large potatoes, cubed
1 cup cubed carrots
2 T chopped fresh parsley
1 28-oz can unsalted diced tomatoes, including juice
2 cup low-sodium GF chicken or vegetable broth
½ lb raw shrimp, peeled and deveined
½ lb raw cod or other white fish cut in bite-size chunks
½ cup dry white wine
Juice of half a lemon
1 t pepper

1. Sauté the onion, shallot, and celery until soft in the oil in a Dutch oven over medium-high heat.
2. Add the potatoes, carrots, parsley, tomatoes, broth and simmer until the carrots and potatoes are soft, about 15 to 20 minutes.
3. Add the uncooked shrimp and white fish.
4. Add the wine and lemon juice and cook the soup for another 5 to 7 minutes, until the seafood is cooked. The shrimp will be pink.
5. Serve immediately.

NUTRITIONAL STATS Servings 6, Serving size 504 g, Calories 280, Calories from fat 50, Fat 6 g, Saturated fat .5 g, Cholesterol 75 mg, Sodium 200 mg, Carbohydrate 33 g, Fiber 4 g, Protein 20 g

Chicken or Turkey Stock for Soup

Read labels carefully when buying commercial stock. Only a few are gluten-free and many contain significant amounts of sodium. But stock that is both gluten-free and low in sodium is available in most grocery stores.

Making your own stock is for the cooking purist. But we recommend it because, once you get the hang if it, it is easy and allows you to have frozen stock on hand. You will need a large stockpot and several hours of time that allows you to check in on the simmering stock. Stock from scratch also requires handling bird carcasses or bones—which some cooks find unpleasant. Typically, I cook up a batch of soup stock on a free Sunday afternoon, maybe after a big Sunday poultry meal. Or I start the stock after work and finish up before bedtime.

Turkey or chicken bones from carcass or 4 turkey wings
1 cup celery, chopped
1 large white onion, chopped
1 cup carrots, chopped
2 t pepper
2 T canola oil
3 T fresh parsley (optional, will make stock look greenish)

1. In a large stockpot over medium-high heat, sauté the vegetables in the oil.
2. Add the bones and 2 to 3 quarts of water. Bring to a boil.
3. Turn down heat and simmer, covered for about 3 hours, until the meat bits fall off the bones.
4. Remove the stock from the heat and let it cool.
5. Discard the bones, skin and mushy vegetables. Set any chunks of meat aside for chicken salad or soup. Strain the broth through a colander into a large bowl. Freeze stock in 1- to 2-cup containers. If you prefer really clear stock, strain it through cheesecloth.

Salads

While soups are one way to combat a cold Wisconsin winter, salads spell refreshing relief during our hot, muggy summers. You can prepare salads early on a summer morning before the heat of the day and chill them in the refrigerator to enjoy later. The best part of salads is that they encourage creative thinking and experimenting—an important element of the cooking practiced in Lepeska-Fitzsimmons family kitchens.

IFC TIP

Make your own dressings

It is not easy to find good-tasting, GF, DF and diabetic-friendly commercial salad dressings. And a good salad really needs a tasty dressing. We almost always make our own following quick and easy recipes. Homemade dressing stores for up to a week in the refrigerator, just shake well before using. Experiment with your favorite oils, vinegars and seasonings to create unique flavors. Use a hand blender or a tightly sealed container to mix the dressing thoroughly.

Basic Vinaigrette

The general guide for basic vinaigrette dressing is one part vinegar to three parts oil. We list one to two teaspoons of sugar as an optional ingredient. Feedback from our recipe testers indicates most people find a dressing without any sugar too tart. Experiment and prepare yours to suit individual palates.

¼ cup white wine vinegar
1 t GF mustard
1 shallot minced, or substitute 1 or more garlic cloves
½ t salt
1 t freshly ground pepper
1-2 t sugar, optional
¾ cup olive oil

1. Combine all ingredients but the olive oil and mix well.
2. Slowly add the olive oil and whisk until emulsified.
3. Enjoy on cleaned, dried salad greens or spinach.

NUTRITIONAL STATS Servings 10, Serving size 26 g, Calories 160, Calories from fat 150, Fat 17 g, Saturated fat 2.5 g, Cholesterol 0 mg, Sodium 240 mg, Carbohydrate 1 g, Fiber 0 mg, Protein 0g

ALTERNATIVES Let your creative side go wild when it comes to salad dressings. Here are some of our favorite variations on the basic theme. These alternatives all contain a sweetener so leave out the additional sugar.

Sweet and Sour Instead of the sugar, sweeten with two tablespoons of real maple syrup, orange marmalade or strawberry jam. The strawberry jam version is great as a dressing on spinach salad with fresh strawberries or raspberries in the spring.

Tangy Citrus Substitute half the vinegar for freshly squeezed lemon juice or lime juice. Use two to three tablespoons of orange marmalade as the sweetener. Add a can of well-drained orange segments, sliced spring onions and a handful of toasted nuts to the salad greens.

Become a pepper snob

We always recommend using freshly ground pepper. Because there are so many things intolerant eaters need to avoid, we think it is okay to be a pepper snob. There are many varieties and colors of peppercorns so you can experiment with many different options. Splurge on a good pepper mill and go grind up some special tastes.

Taco Salad

FASTER THAN TAKE-OUT

1 lb lean ground beef
1 small white onion, chopped
1 clove garlic, minced
2 t chili powder
1 t cumin
1 t oregano
1 14-oz can low-sodium diced tomatoes
6 cups salad greens, washed and dried
1 bag GF corn chips
1 avocado, peeled, pitted and mashed, and mixed with
    ½ cup GF salsa
1 16-oz jar GF salsa, optional

Toppings
2 tomatoes cut into thin slices
¾ cup shredded carrots
2 spring onions, white parts only, sliced crosswise
¼ cup sliced ripe or green olives

1. Brown the beef in a frying pan over medium high heat with the onion and garlic
2. Stir in the chili powder, cumin and oregano.
3. Drain off any extra fat and add the canned tomatoes with their juice.
4. Cover and simmer for about 15 minutes. Most of the juice will evaporate.
5. Place the salad greens in a big bowl or divide between four individual plates.
6. Arrange the fresh tomatoes, spring onion, carrots, and olives on top of greens.
7. Mash the avocado in a small bowl and add ½ cup of GF salsa. Place a scoop of avocado in the center of each serving and put a quarter of the meat around the avocado.
8. Serve with GF chips and additional GF salsa.

NUTRITIONAL STATS Servings 4, Serving size 471 g, Calories 310, Calories from fat 120, Fat 14 g, Saturated fat 3 g, Cholesterol 60 mg, Sodium 680 mg, Carbohydrate 21 g, Fiber 9 g, Protein 25 g

Note: Nutritional stats do not include corn chips.

Chef's Salad FTT

FASTER THAN TAKE-OUT

A traditional chef's salad is an excellent way to use odds and ends in the refrigerator. Since prepared lunchmeats often present a problem for intolerant eaters, leftover roasts or grilled meats from the freezer make great chef's salad ingredients.

6-8 cups salad greens, cleaned and dried
2 cups meat strips, leftover roasts such as turkey, beef or pork work well
2 tomatoes sliced in vertical slices
1 cup shredded carrots
2 hard cooked eggs

Other choices for salad toppings:
¼ cup sliced olives
¼ cup chopped radishes
½ cup thinly sliced, peeled cucumbers
½ cup green or red pepper strips

1. Place the salad greens in large bowl or individual serving plates.
2. Arrange the meats and vegetables attractively on top of the greens.
3. Drizzle vinaigrette over the salad and serve cold.

NUTRITIONAL STATS Servings 4, Serving size 359 g, Calories 250, Calories from fat 70, Fat 7 g, Saturated fat 2 g, Cholesterol 180 mg, Sodium 210 mg, Carbohydrate 13 g, Fiber 5 g, Protein 33 g

Note: Nutritional stats do not include dressing.

Curried Shrimp and Quinoa or Spinach Salad

These next two salads use the same curried shrimp. Combine the shrimp with spinach and potatoes for an excellent light summer salad or use it to top off a quinoa salad for a seasonal change of pace.

1 lb raw large shrimp, shelled and deveined
2 T canola oil
½ T curry powder
1 T fresh minced fresh ginger or 1 t powdered ginger
1 shallot or 1 small onion, thinly sliced
1 t pepper

1. Place the oil in a sauté pan over medium heat.
2. Add the curry powder, ginger and shallot or onion and sauté for about 2 minutes.
3. Add the shrimp and sauté until pink and cooked through for about 5 minutes more, stirring occasionally.
4. Place cooked shrimp in a storage container, pour any extra juice from the pan over the shrimp and refrigerate.

NUTRITIONAL STATS Servings 4, Serving size 385 g, Calories 480, Calories from fat 210, Fat 24 g, Saturated fat 2 g, Cholesterol 170 mg, Sodium 420 mg, Carbohydrate 34 g, Fiber 3 g, Protein 31 g

Spinach and Shrimp Salad

4-6 cups cleaned spinach
4 medium potatoes
Curried shrimp, *see pg 45*
Citris Dressing

1. Place potatoes in a large saucepan and cover with water.
2. Cover, simmer the potatoes for 30 minutes or until tender.
3. Drain the potatoes and immerse them in a bowl of ice water. When the potatoes are cool, peel and slice.
4. Marinate the potatoes in a ½ cup of citrus dressing for 2 hours or more.
5. Place greens on a serving plate and arrange row of potato slices on each side. Arrange shrimp down the center. Drizzle with additional dressing and serve.

NUTRITIONAL STATS Servings 4, Serving size 287 g, Calories 240, Calories from fat 80, Fat 9 g, Saturated fat 1 g, Cholesterol 170 mg, Sodium 820 mg, Carbohydrate 14 g, Fiber 5 g, Protein 27 g

Citrus Dressing

¼ cup lemon juice
2 T orange marmalade
Zest of one lemon
1 t GF mustard
1 shallot, minced
1 t salt
1 t pepper
¾ cup extra virgin olive oil

1. Combine all the ingredients except the oil in a blender and mix until well combined.
2. Slowly add the olive oil until the dressing is blended.

NUTRITIONAL STATS Servings 12, Serving size 29 g, Calories 140, Calories from fat 130, Fat 14 g, Saturated fat 2 g, Cholesterol 0 mg, Sodium 200 mg, Carbohydrate 4 g, Fiber 0 g, Protein 0 g

Cooking your own shrimp worth the effort

Cooked shrimp is easily available and handy in salad prep, but it is worth the extra effort to cook the shrimp yourself. Except near coastal waters, fresh shrimp is difficult to obtain. Most grocery stores carry raw frozen shrimp. This works fine, as does raw shrimp that comes peeled and deveined. To shell and devein the shrimp yourself, remove the shells and use a sharp knife to remove the vein that runs along the back of the shrimp. Some stores carry easy-peel shrimp with the shell split and the vein removed, a real time saver. Rinse your hands in lemon water to remove the fishy smell.

Quinoa and Shrimp Salad

1 cup quinoa, uncooked
2 cups water
4 radishes, sliced thinly
2 spring onions, sliced thinly
½ cup red or green pepper, chopped
Curried shrimp, *see pg 45*
Cucumber Dressing

1. Place quinoa and water in a covered saucepan.
2. Bring to a boil and then reduce heat to a simmer. Simmer for 15 minutes, until water is absorbed and grain appears translucent then remove from heat and let it cool.
3. When the quinoa is cool, add the radishes, onions and pepper.
4. Toss with the cucumber dressing retaining 2 tablespoons of the dressing.
5. Place salad on a serving platter and top with the shrimp.
6. Drizzle the remaining dressing over the shrimp.

Cucumber Dressing

Also a good dipping sauce for shrimp appetizers.

1 English cucumber, halved lengthwise and chopped, or
   1 regular cucumber, peeled with seeds removed or
   4 small farm-fresh cucumbers, peeled with seeds removed
¼ cup unseasoned rice vinegar
1 T sesame oil
2 T sesame seeds
2 t fish sauce
2 T canola oil
1 or more t freshly ground pepper

1. Puree cucumber with vinegar in blender until smooth.
2. Add the remaining ingredients and blend until all ingredients are combined.

NUTRITIONAL STATS Servings 4, Serving size 385 g, Calories 480, Calories from fat 210, Fat 24 g, Saturated fat 2 g, Cholesterol 170 mg, Sodium 420 mg, Carbohydrate 34 g, Fiber 3 g, Protein 31 g

Note: Nutritional stats include shrimp, quinoa and dressing.

Try versatile quinoa

IFC TIP

Quinoa is a quick and easy GF grain-like food that is nutritious and easy to prepare. Enjoy it warm or use it as an excellent GF base for cold salads. Substitute quinoa for bulgur in your favorite tabouli recipe or try it in place of rice in almost any dish. Quinoa flakes make an excellent breatfast cereal and addition to baking.

Curried Chicken or Turkey Salad

This is a simple do-ahead summer main-course salad. Cook boneless skinless chicken breasts or a turkey breast the day before and assemble the salad early on the day you plan to serve it. The salad is best when the flavors have a chance to blend. Stir in the nuts immediately before serving.

3 cups cooked chicken or turkey, cut in bite-size pieces
1½ cups green grapes, sliced in half
1 cup jicama cut in thin strips or 1 can water chestnuts, drained and sliced
1 red pepper, chopped
½ cup GF mayonnaise
¼ cup white wine or cider vinegar
½ T curry
1 t freshly ground pepper
½ cup roasted walnut pieces, reserving 1 T
6-8 cups of salad greens

1. Place the chicken, grapes, jicama and red pepper in a large bowl.
2. In a small bowl, combine the mayonnaise with the vinegar, curry and pepper. Whisk to combine.
3. Pour the dressing over the chicken salad and gently stir to combine the ingredients. Prepare to this point and refrigerate if making ahead.
4. Stir in the roasted nuts when the salad is ready to serve.
5. Place the greens in a large salad bowl and top with the chicken salad. Garnish with the reserved walnuts.

NUTRITIONAL STATS Servings 6, Serving size 238 g, Calories 360, Calories from fat 210, Fat 24 g, Saturated fat 2 g, Cholesterol 55 mg, Sodium 190 mg, Carbohydrate 14 g, Fiber 4 g, Protein 24 g

What is jicama?

Jicama is a firm, slightly sweet root vegetable sometimes used in Mexican cooking or as an ingredient in a stir-fry. In the grocery story, it is often located near the hot peppers. Jicama has a firm texture that stays crisp even when cooked. It makes an unusual addition to a tray of veggies and a crunchy ingredient in salads. Store at room temperature before you use it. To prepare, peel off the thin brown skin and slice. Keep leftover jicama in the refrigerator for later use. Sprinkle with lime and chili powder for a tasty treat.

open when it is cooked. You can prepare the rice ahead and refrigerate.

3. Toast the walnuts on a baking sheet for 10 minutes at 300°. Set aside to cool when toasted.
4. Place the rest of the ingredients in a large bowl and refrigerate. Combine all ingredients, except the nuts, with the dressing and refrigerate until time to serve. Add nuts immediately before serving.

NUTRITIONAL STATS Servings 6, Serving size 256 g, Calories 310, Calories from fat 50, Fat 6 g, Saturated fat 1 g, Cholesterol 30 mg, Sodium 210 mg, Carbohydrate 44 g, Fiber 4 g, Protein 23 g

Note: Nutritional stats represent a salad of wild rice, turkey, walnuts, asparagus, red pepper and cranberries.

Wild Rice Dressing

¼ cup white wine vinegar
1 T minced shallots
1 t GF mustard
¼ cup real maple syrup
¾ cup olive oil

Blend all ingredients except oil. Slowly drizzle in the oil until well blended.

NUTRITIONAL STATS Servings 6, Serving size 54 g, Calories 290, Calories from fat 250, Fat 28 g, Saturated fat 4 g, Cholesterol 0 mg, Sodium 10 mg, Carbohydrate 9 g, Fiber 0 g, Protein 0 g

 IFC TIP

Leftover wild rice comes in handy

Wild rice takes longer to prepare than white rice and expands to create more cooked rice. Save leftover wild rice for later use by placing the unused portion in a freezer container and slipping it into the freezer. When planning your next soup or salad, this ready-cooked ingredient adds its nutty, chewy flavor to many combinations.

Shredded Carrot Salads

I like carrots and think we overlook them too often as a great vegetable salad ingredient. The next four recipes are variations on the theme of shredded carrot salads. Serve them as they are or on top of mixed salad greens. You can shred your own carrots or, for quick meals, buy shredded carrots in the grocery. Pre-shredded carrots in 10-ounce bags are equivalent to about four regular carrots. Since most children like carrots, carrot salads are a good way to get youngsters to increase fruits, vegetables and fiber in their diet.

Carrot Walnut Salad

10-oz bag of shredded carrots
½ cup walnuts
½ cup raisins, golden raisins are the best
½ cup GF prepared mayonnaise
¼ cup white wine vinegar or cider vinegar
1 t or more freshly ground pepper
½ t salt

1. Toast the walnuts in a 300° oven for 10 minutes. Place the carrots and raisins in a serving bowl.
2. Mix the mayonnaise, vinegar and salt and pepper together.
3. Pour the dressing over the carrots and raisins. Refrigerate at this point if planning to serve later. Mix in the toasted nuts immediately before serving.

NUTRITIONAL STATS Servings 6, Serving size 100 g, Calories 260, Calories from fat 190, Fat 21 g, Saturated fat 1.5 g, Cholesterol 5 mg, Sodium 350 mg, Carbohydrate 17 g, Fiber 3 g, Protein 2 g

Orange Carrot Salad

An oil-free version with a tang.

10-oz bag of shredded carrots
Grated zest of one orange
Juice of one large orange
Juice of one large lemon
½ t salt
2 T powdered sugar

1. Place the shredded carrots in a bowl.
2. Whisk together the remaining ingredients and pour the dressing over the carrots.

3. You can serve immediately, but salad is best when chilled for at least 1 hour in the refrigerator. Or prepare ahead and refrigerate overnight in an airtight container.

NUTRITIONAL STATS Servings 4, Serving size 106 g, Calories 50, Calories from fat 0, Fat 0g, Saturated fat 0 g, Cholesterol 0 mg, Sodium 340 mg, Carbohydrate 13 g, Fiber 2 g, Protein 1 g

Carrot Salad with Lime and Cilantro

1 10-oz bag of shredded carrots
1 T fresh lime juice
Zest from half a lime
¼ cup finely chopped fresh cilantro
Additional cilantro sprigs for garnish
2 T extra virgin olive oil
½ t salt
1 t pepper

1. Place the shredded carrots in a bowl.
2. Mix the lime juice, zest, chopped cilantro, and salt and pepper together and slowly blend in the oil.
3. Pour the dressing over the carrots and serve garnished with cilantro sprigs.

NUTRITIONAL STATS Servings 6, Serving size 56 g, Calories 60, Calories from fat 40, Fat 5 g, Saturated fat 0 g, Cholesterol 0 mg, Sodium 230 mg, Carbohydrate 5 g, Fiber 1 g, Protein 1 g

Carrot and Pineapple Salad

1 10-oz bag of shredded carrots
¼ cup chopped cilantro
½ cup crushed pineapple canned in its own juice, drained, reserving juice
2 T pineapple juice from canned pineapple
2 T canola oil
2 t sesame oil
½ t salt
1 t pepper

1. Place the carrots, well-drained pineapple and cilantro into a medium bowl.
2. Blend the pineapple juice, oils, salt, pepper until well mixed.
3. Pour over carrots. This salad is best when made in advance.

NUTRITIONAL STATS Servings 6, Serving size 76 g, Calories 90, Calories from fat 60, Fat 6 g, Saturated fat .5 g, Cholesterol 0 mg, Sodium 35 mg, Carbohydrate 8 g, Fiber 2 g, Protein 1 g

Roasted Tomato and Grilled Red Pepper Salad

This salad is fussy but so good it is worth the effort and makes a great match for greens, GF pasta or quinoa. Look for variations on it in the *Starters* chapter where you will find other interesting ways to combine roasted tomatoes and grilled peppers for pâtés and dips. You can prepare the peppers and tomatoes early in the day or put the entire salad together a day ahead and refrigerate overnight.

4 red bell peppers
10-15 Roma tomatoes
3-4 cloves garlic, sliced
½ cup extra virgin olive oil, divided
10–15 leaves of fresh basil, roughly chopped
1 t kosher salt
1-2 t freshly ground pepper
¼ cup red wine or balsamic vinegar
6 cups substantial salad greens such as romaine or 6 cups of prepared GF pasta

Optional adds:
½ cup ripe olives
1 cup sliced artichoke hearts

1. Roast the red bell peppers. Instructions on pg.16.
2. Place the tomatoes, garlic and chopped basil on the jelly roll pan.
3. Drizzle with 1 to 2 tablespoons of olive oil, then sprinkle with salt and lots of pepper. Cook for 45 minutes in a 400º oven until the tomatoes are somewhat shriveled.
4. While the tomatoes bake, check on the peppers. Once cool, the charred skin blisters and is easy to remove. Slice the peppers in thin strips.
5. Remove the tomatoes, garlic and basil from the oven when ready and place in a bowl with the pepper strips.
6. Scrape the juice and oil that remains on the pan into the bowl. Add the drained artichoke hearts or olives, if used.
7. Combine the remaining olive oil with the vinegar and whisk together. Pour the dressing over the vegetables. Refrigerate to allow the flavors to blend.

Serving Options:
Place the salad greens, the cooked pasta or quinoa in a large salad bowl. Top with the marinated vegetables and toss before serving. Also try arranging the vegetables on a plate as part of an antipasto tray.

NUTRITIONAL STATS Servings 10, Serving size 130 g, Calories 130, Calories from fat 100, Fat 11 g, Saturated fat 1.5 g, Cholesterol 0 mg, Sodium 240 mg, Carbohydrate 7 g, Fiber 2 g, Protein 1 g

Asparagus with Tarragon Vinaigrette

1½ lbs asparagus, woody ends removed
4–6 cup cleaned, dried salad greens

Dressing
1 T cider vinegar
2 t minced shallot
1 t mustard
¼ t salt
1/8 t black pepper or more
3 T olive oil
1½ t finely chopped fresh tarragon
1-2 t sugar, optional
1 hard-cooked egg, chopped

1. Steam asparagus until just tender, 3 to 5 minutes.
2. Immediately transfer to a bowl of ice water to stop cooking.
3. Drain well and pat dry.
4. Blend together vinegar, shallots, mustard, tarragon, sugar, salt and pepper, and add oil in a slow stream until dressing is well blended.
5. Place salad greens on a serving plate or individual salad plates. Put the asparagus on top of the greens and drizzle the dressing over the top. Garnish with the chopped egg.

NUTRITIONAL STATS Servings 6, Serving size 192 g, Calories 110, Calories from fat 70, Fat 8 g, Saturated fat 1.5 g, Cholesterol 35 mg, Sodium 140 mg, Carbohydrate 8 g, Fiber 4 g, Protein 4 g

Cucumber Salads

Almost everyone likes cucumbers and whenever we prepare a cucumber salad, there are no leftovers. These cucumber recipes call for English cucumbers. In the grocery, they are the ones wrapped in cellophane. If you have fresh-from-the-garden cucumbers, even better. But they are not available all year round, at least not here in the upper Midwest. Small, fresh cucumbers are the tastiest so find them where you can in season—from your neighbor's garden, at farmers' markets and in some grocery stores.

Sweet and Sour Cucumbers with Fresh Dill

2 English cucumbers, peeled and sliced very thin
1 t kosher salt
½ cup white wine vinegar
¼ cup chopped fresh dill
2 T sugar
½ t freshly ground black pepper

1. Place the cucumber slices in a colander and sprinkle with salt; toss to coat. Let stand 15 minutes, stirring occasionally. Liquid will seep out the bottom so place the colander over a bigger bowl or in the sink.
2. Stir vinegar, dill, sugar and pepper in a large bowl until the sugar dissolves.
3. Shake the liquid off the cucumber slices and place them in a serving dish.
4. Add the dressing and stir to blend.
5. Refrigerate at least 15 minutes and up to 2 hours. Serve cold.

NUTRITIONAL STATS Servings 6, Serving size 118 g, Calories 25, Calories from Fat 0, Saturated fat 0 g, Cholesterol 0 mg, Sodium 390 mg, Carbohydrate 5 g, Fiber 1 g, Protein 1 g

Ginger Cukes

2 English cucumbers peeled and sliced
1 T fresh ginger, minced
1 jalapeno pepper, minced
½ t salt
1 t freshly grated pepper
1 T honey
Juice of one lemon

1. Peel the cucumbers and slice thinly. Add the ginger and pepper.
2. Whisk together the remaining ingredients and pour over the cucumbers.
3. Refrigerate for 2 hours or overnight. Serve cold.

NUTRITIONAL STATS Servings 6, Serving size 111 g, Calories 30, Calories from fat 0, Fat 0 g, Saturated fat 0 g, Cholesterol 0 mg, Sodium 200 mg, Carbohydrate 6 g, Fiber 1 g, Protein 1 g

Peanut Cole Slaw

This slaw is a change-of-pace from mayo-based cole slaws. You can make the recipe ahead of time and, because it works well for a crowd, double or triple it successfully. I did not really appreciate this slaw until I got an email from Molly one day when she lived in Portland, Oregon. She asked me to send the recipe so she could forward it to a friend in Ireland who wanted to make the slaw that day for her new husband's Irish family. Thanks to the wonders of modern communications, Peanut Cole Slaw went from Wisconsin to Oregon to Ireland in a matter of minutes.

4 cups thinly sliced or shredded cabbage
1-2 cups shredded carrots
1 cup salted peanuts, reserve 3 T for garnish

Dressing
½ cup canola oil
¼ cup unseasoned rice vinegar or cider vinegar
1 T sesame oil
2 t freshly ground pepper
1 T sugar

1. Place the cabbage and carrots in a large serving bowl.
2. Whisk the vinegar, sesame oil, pepper and sugar together, and slowly add the canola oil, blending the mixture until combined.
3. Pour the dressing over the cabbage.
4. Add the peanuts right before serving, garnish with the 3 tablespoons set aside.

NUTRITIONAL STATS Servings 10, Serving size 97 g, Calories 240, Calories from fat 190, Fat 21 g, Saturated fat 3 g, Cholesterol 0 mg, Sodium 120 mg, Carbohydrate 8 g, Fiber 3 g, Protein 5 g

Frizzled Leek Salad

MOLLY RECALLS: The first time I had frizzled leaks was at one of those expensive toss-your-own salad places in New York City. I didn't know what a frizzled leak was (fried by Snoop Dog, maybe?). But I did know it was delicious. I made up a recipe and introduced it to the family. The frizzled leeks add texture and a little *naughty* to a healthy salad.

2 large leeks, cleaned and sliced lengthwise in thin slices, white part only
¾ cup olive oil
8 cups salad greens, cleaned
4 Roma tomatoes, quartered
1 red or 1 yellow pepper, grilled, skins removed and sliced in thin slices
2 green onions, sliced white parts only
1 cup canned sliced beets, drained and cut in thin strips, or 2-3 small fresh beets, roasted, cooled with skins removed
¼ cup unsalted sunflower seeds, shelled and roasted
1 clove garlic, minced
3 T white wine vinegar
1 t GF mustard
2 t sugar
1 t salt
1 t pepper

1. Place the olive oil in a frying pan and heat to medium-high. Add the thinly sliced leeks and fry until they are light brown and frizzled, about 8 to 10 minutes.
2. Remove the leeks from the oil and drain on a paper towel. Cool the oil to use for the dressing.
3. While the oil is cooling, assemble the greens, pepper, onion, tomatoes, beets and sunflower seeds in a large bowl.
4. Whisk the vinegar, mustard, garlic, sugar, salt and pepper.
5. Measure the oil that remains from frizzling the leeks. Add additional oil if needed to have 2/3 cup of oil.
6. Slowly add the oil to the vinegar mixture and blend until dressing is mixed.
7. Add 2 tablespoons frizzled leeks to the dressing and blend for an additional few seconds.
8. Pour dressing over the salad and top with the prepared frizzled leeks.

NUTRITIONAL STATS Servings 8, Serving size 159 g, Calories 240, Calories from fat 210, Fat 23 g, Saturated fat 3 g, Cholesterol 0 mg, Sodium 350 mg, Carbohydrate 9 g, Fiber 3 g, Protein 2 g

Main Courses

MOLLY REFLECTS: When you are on a restrictive diet, like a gluten- and dairy- free diet, or watching your carbohydrates, sometimes you feel like your whole diet is a substitution for the real thing. One of the great things about meat is that, in its natural state, it is gluten-free, dairy-free, low in carbohydrates and, in a pinch, you can prepare it without much embellishment. We find that when traveling as a family, steak or seafood restaurants are excellent "go to" choices if we're unsure about how accommodating restaurants will be—as long as the chef is willing to prepare one of the steaks WELL done since Mom doesn't like anything red on her meat plate!

By all accounts, we are what you would call a traditional meat-eating family. Not in the way that we are all ravenous carnivores. Typically, we stay within the realm of traditional meats, like chicken, beef, pork and fish. But just because you stay in the traditional realm, it doesn't mean that what you eat can't be exotic and flavorful!

Within this *Main Courses* chapter, you'll find some of our favorite meat recipes, both old favorites and new ones we've picked up along the way. If you have more exotic tastes in meat, please feel free to substitute as you see fit.

Turkey Barbeque

This recipe is perfect for potlucks and informal suppers for a group. I feel more confident eating food at potlucks that I prepare myself—this was true even before I became intolerant—so I always want to make and take something exceptionally good. Now, of course, it is unwise to eat food without knowing exactly what is in it and how it was prepared. This turkey dish always is a big hit and a recipe people often ask me to share.

2 large onions, chopped
1-2 large garlic cloves, peeled and minced
2 cups cider vinegar
½ cup GF ketchup
A few dried hot peppers or 1-3 t cayenne or other hot pepper
1 T salt
1 T freshly ground black pepper
1 4½ -5 lb turkey breast, skin discarded.

1. Place onions, garlic, vinegar, ketchup, salt and pepper in a Dutch oven or stockpot and simmer covered for 15 minutes.
2. Add the turkey breast and simmer for 2½ hours. Check every 20 minutes to make sure turkey doesn't stick to bottom of pan. If it does, reduce the heat.
3. Take the turkey out of the liquid and cool on a cutting board. When cool enough to handle, shred the turkey meat or cut in slices, removing and discarding the bones and any remaining skin.
4. Place the meat back in the broth and simmer for an additional 1 to 2 hours. Add additional water, one cup at time, if necessary.
5. Season with additional salt, pepper and hot pepper as desired. Serve the meat as is or as sandwiches with GF bread or buns. The leftovers freeze well and taste good reheated.

NUTRITIONAL STATS Servings 16, Serving size 183 g, Calories 170, Calories from fat 30, Fat 3.5 g, Saturated fat 1 g, Cholesterol 85 mg, Sodium 160 mg, Carbohydrate 1 g, Fiber 0 g, Protein 30 g

Not Your Mother's Pot Roasted Chicken or Beef

When I was growing up in a small town in Wisconsin, Sunday was often pot-roast day. Beef or chicken, my mother baked the roast in a pot with potatoes and carrots. This variation on the Sunday pot roast is a little spicier than what my mother used to make.

1 roasting chicken or a 2 lb boneless beef round roast
4 large cloves garlic, coarsely chopped
1 t kosher salt and 1t pepper
½ cup fresh cilantro, chopped
1 T ancho chili powder or 2 t chipotle, for a smokier flavor
2 t cumin
2 T olive oil
1 lb medium carrots, halved and cut in chunks.
1 lb potatoes cut in chunks or use small red potatoes
1 rutabaga, peeled and cut in chunks (optional: rutabaga is an acquired taste)

1. Preheat oven to 350º.
2. Rinse meat and season with salt and pepper.
3. Mash garlic to a paste with salt. Add cilantro, chili powder, cumin and oil, and stir to blend.
4. Rub the seasoning paste under the skin of the breast and thighs and in the inside cavity of the bird. Or rub the seasoning lightly over the entire beef roast.
5. Put the meat in a covered roasting pan. Bake covered for 1 hour.
6. Add the potatoes and carrots and rutabaga, if used.
7. Pour about 1 inch of water over the vegetables. Cover the pan and roast for an additional hour. Remove the cover and cook approximately 15 more minutes so the meat browns. Beef should be tender. Chicken should register 170 degrees on a meat thermometer inserted into the thigh. Baste occasionally with juice from bottom of pan.
8. Transfer the meat and vegetables to a serving platter and keep warm.
9. Pour any juice in the bottom of the pan into a bowl and serve with meat and vegetables, or make gravy by adding 1 tablespoon cornstarch mixed in a ½ cup water to the simmering pan juices. Continue simmering until the gravy is thickened.

NUTRITIONAL STATS Servings 6, Serving size 342 g, Calories 410, Calories from fat 110, Fat 12 g, Saturated fat 3 g, Cholesterol 90 mg, Sodium 500 mg, Carbohydrate 27 g, Fiber 5 g, Protein 46 g

Note: Nutritional stats represent beef round roast.

Lemon Chicken with Ripe and Green Olives

Because you can marinate this recipe ahead of time, it is a good choice for entertaining. Double or triple for a crowd.

4 boneless, skinless chicken breasts
¼ cup olive oil
1 T turmeric
1-2 t powdered ginger or 1 T sliced fresh ginger
2 cloves garlic, minced
1 medium onion, sliced
¼ cup chopped fresh parsley or 1 T dried
¼ cup chopped fresh cilantro or 1 T dried
2 lemons, 1 in slices
¼ cup mixed pitted ripe and green olives

1. Prepare marinade by putting the juice of one lemon, olive oil, turmeric, ginger, garlic, sliced onion, parsley and cilantro in a medium bowl, stir to combine.
2. Place chicken breasts in a flat dish or sealable plastic bag.
3. Pour the marinade over chicken and marinate at least 2 hours or overnight, turning often.
4. When ready to bake, preheat the oven to 375º.
5. Place the meat in a baking dish. Cut the second lemon into slices and sprinkle the lemon slices and the olives over the chicken.
6. Bake for 40 minutes or until chicken is cooked through.
7. Place the chicken on a serving platter. Spoon the lemon slices and olives with the pan juices over the chicken. Serve with rice.

NUTRITIONAL STATS Servings 4, Serving size 184 g, Calories 310, Calories from fat 160, Fat 18 g, Saturated fat 3 g, Cholesterol 75 mg, Sodium 140 mg, Carbohydrate 9 g, Fiber 2 g, Protein 28 g

IFC TIP

Try saffron for a unique flavor

Substitute a large pinch of saffron for the turmeric to experience a different flavor. Saffron is an expensive spice and not available in all grocery stores. But it brings a unique and interesting quality to food. If using saffron in the Lemon Chicken recipe, steep it in a half-cup of boiling water for 15 minutes and then add to the marinade.

Molly's First Thanksgiving or Chicken Enchiladas with Salsa Verde

MOLLY RECALLS: Mom likes to call this recipe "Molly's first Thanksgiving." My junior year in college, I decided it was time to cut the umbilical cord and stay at school for Thanksgiving. One of my roommates stayed and we convinced a great friend who graduated the year before to come back and enjoy a beautiful warm fall Thanksgiving in Austin, Texas. Being the non-traditionalist I am, I decided that a great alternative to the boring old turkey dinner was Turkey Enchiladas with Salsa Verde. The recipe here is for chicken, but you can substitute turkey or beans. For those who tolerate dairy, this recipe also is good with two cups of shredded cheese. We sometimes make a pan with cheese and a smaller pan without cheese.

Tomatillo Sauce
⅓ cup oil
2 medium onions, chopped
1 small can diced chilies
3 cups fresh tomatillos, husked, washed and sliced
1 cup GF chicken stock
3 T lime juice
2 t oregano
1 t cumin

1. In a large saucepan over medium heat, sauté the onions in the oil.
2. Add the chilies, tomatillos, stock, lime juice, oregano and cumin.
3. Simmer for 25 minutes.
4. Puree in a blender or with a hand blender.

Enchiladas
4 cups cooked chicken or turkey, shredded
1 can diced chilies
1½ t oregano
½ cup fresh cilantro, chopped
1 cup tomatillo sauce
12 GF corn tortillas
2 cups shredded cheddar cheese, optional

1. Spray a 9 x 13 inch baking pan with cooking spray.
2. Combine cooked poultry, 1 cup of cheese (if used), chilies, oregano, cilantro and 1 cup tomatillo sauce in bowl.
3. Place chicken mixture in center of a tortilla and roll up. Place the rolled tortilla in the baking dish.
4. Repeat until all tortillas are rolled and in the baking dish.
5. If baking right away, top with additional sauce and

additional cup of cheese, if used.
6. If baking later, cover and refrigerate without topping with additional sauce. Add sauce right before baking.
7. Bake uncovered in a 350° oven for 45 minutes, or until the enchiladas are hot and bubbly.

NUTRITIONAL STATS Servings 12, Serving size 193 g, Calories 200, Calories from fat 80, Fat 9 g, Saturated fat 1 g, Cholesterol 40 mg, Sodium 160 mg, Carbohydrate 13 g, Fiber 2 g, Protein 17 g

Note: Nutritional stats do not include cheese.

Chicken Pasta Dinner

FASTER THAN TAKE-OUT

This is a good odds-and-ends dish. Instead of sun-dried tomatoes, try adding carrot strips, sliced zucchini or other veggies you find in your refrigerator. Keep the spinach for color, and the olives for a salty zing, but feel free to experiment with the other vegetables.

2 shallots, peeled and chopped
2 T olive oil
1 lb boneless skinless chicken breasts, sliced into smaller pieces
1 t paprika
1 t cumin
1 t pepper
1 cup white wine
½ cup sun-dried tomatoes
4 cups spinach, well cleaned
10 sliced green olives

1. In a large frying pan over medium heat, sauté the shallots in olive oil until wilted.
2. Add chicken pieces, paprika, cumin and pepper, and cook until chicken browns.
3. Add the wine and tomatoes, cover and simmer for 20 minutes.
4. Add the spinach and olives and cook uncovered for an additional 2 minutes.
5. Serve over GF pasta or rice.

NUTRITIONAL STATS Servings 4, Serving size 189 g, Calories 290, Calories from fat 110, Fat 12 g, Saturated fat 2 g, Cholesterol 65 mg, Sodium 440 mg, Carbohydrate 10 g, Fiber 2 g, Protein 25 g

Chicken Satay with Peanut Sauce

After Molly and Gregg married, they invited us for a fancy dinner to thank us for hosting their wedding. They prepared this recipe and Beef Wrapped in Lettuce, recipe pg. 69. Since then, I frequently use both entrees for buffets and gatherings.

¼ cup canola oil
¼ cup lemon juice
1 T freshly grated ginger or 1 t powdered ginger
1 T minced garlic
1 T curry powder, less if you prefer
2 lbs skinless, boneless chicken breasts cut into strips or chicken tenders

20 wooden skewers, soaked in water for 20 minutes

1. Prepare the marinade by combining the oil and lemon juice with the ginger, garlic and curry powder in a plastic bag or mixing bowl.
2. Add chicken strips and tightly close the bag.
3. Marinate in the refrigerator for 2 hours or longer.
4. Thread the chicken on wooden skewers.
5. Place the skewers on a baking sheet and broil for 5 minutes a side, 1 to 2 inches from the broiler. Alternately, place meat skewers on a charcoal or gas grill. Serve with Peanut Sauce, recipe pg. 25.

NUTRITIONAL STATS Servings 8, Serving size 91 g, Calories 190, Calories from fat 90, Fat 10 g, Saturated fat 1.5 g, Cholesterol 65 mg, Sodium 55 mg, Carbohydrate 2 g, Fiber 0 g, Protein 23 g

Turkey and Pear Sauté

¼ cup olive oil
2 T dried basil
2 T GF flour or Parmesan cheese
1 t salt
1 lb turkey cutlets
2 T almonds, halved or slivers
2 pears, peeled and thinly sliced
½ cup dry white wine

1. Mix basil and flour or cheese together on a plate.
2. If turkey cutlets are not thin, pound with a mallet until about ½-inch thick.
3. Heat the oil in a frying pan over medium-high heat.
4. Dredge the cutlets in the basil mixture and sauté until golden brown and cooked through. Keep the turkey warm on a covered serving platter.
5. When the meat is done, add the almonds to the pan and lightly toast for 3 to 5 minutes.
6. Remove the almonds and set aside.
7. Add the pears and white wine and cook uncovered, turning fruit, until most of the liquid is absorbed.
8. To serve, place the pears over the turkey cutlets, pour any remaining pan juices over the pears and turkey.
9. Top with the toasted almonds and serve with wild rice or regular rice.

NUTRITIONAL STATS Servings 4, Serving size 250 g, Calories 360, Calories from fat 150, Fat 17 g, Saturated fat 2 g, Cholesterol 45 mg, Sodium 105 mg, Carbohydrate 19 g, Fiber 4 g, Protein 30 g

Tolerating aged Parmesan cheese

Some dairy intolerants tolerate aged Parmesan cheese, which makes it an optional alternative to the GF flour. When substituting Parmesan, grate the cheese from an aged block. Some prepackaged Parmesan products mix new Parmesan cheese with the aged kind, making it less well tolerated.

Curried Beef

The original version of this dish came from a friend who enjoys preparing good food in interesting ways. Because this dish is spicy, we add sweet potatoes to provide a nice balance. Preferring lean cuts of beef, we prepare this recipe using round steak. Round is a less-tender cut so moist-cook it for a longer time. For speedier prep that eliminates the first hour of cooking time, substitute more tender cuts, like sirloin steak cut in strips or flank steak cut on the diagonal.

1 pound round steak cut in thin strips, all fat removed
1 T canola oil
¼ t salt
1 t pepper
1 T fresh ginger, minced or 1 t powdered ginger
1 shallot, minced
1-2 jalapeno peppers, seeded and minced
2 medium red onions, sliced vertically
1 T curry powder
1 t coriander
1 14.5-oz can unsalted diced tomatoes
½ cup coconut milk
3 small sweet potatoes, peeled and cut in chunks
2 cups hot cooked rice, optional

1. Heat the oil in a frying pan over medium heat.
2. Add the steak, salt and pepper, and sauté for 3 or 4 minutes.
3. Add the ginger, shallots, jalapeno pepper and sauté another minute.
4. Add the onion, curry, coriander and tomatoes. Cover and simmer for about an hour and 15 minutes.
5. Add the sweet potato chunks and continue simmering until potatoes and meat are tender, about another 45 minutes.
6. Stir in the coconut milk and cook until the mixture is warm. May be served on cooked rice.

NUTRITIONAL STATS Servings 4, Serving size 410 g, Calories 390, Calories from fat 150, Fat 16 g, Saturated fat 8 g, Cholesterol 70 mg, Sodium 310 mg, Carbohydrate 31 g, Fiber 6 g, Protein 28 g

Beef Wrapped in Lettuce

FASTER THAN TAKE-OUT

This dish is delicious, easy and fun. It is a great addition to a cocktail party buffet or served at an informal dinner party. The lettuce wrap around the meat makes it an excellent choice—both for people who are carb conscious or gluten intolerant. Use Boston, Bibb or other leafy lettuce. Leaves from iceberg lettuce do not work well for wraps. We include a ground turkey filling here as an alternative. These two fillings also work well with the spring rolls recipe in the *Starters* chapter.

1½ lbs extra lean ground beef
1 green pepper, chopped
1 small to medium red onion, chopped
1 clove garlic, chopped
1 T fish sauce
½ cup red wine
1 T freshly grated ginger
1 t turmeric
1 t coriander
1 T cornstarch
¼ cup water
1 cup shredded carrots
1-2 bunches of Boston, Bibb or red leaf lettuce

1. In a large frying pan, over medium heat, brown the beef with onion, pepper and garlic.
2. Drain the excess fat. Add the fish sauce, wine, ginger, turmeric and coriander, and simmer 20 to 30 minutes longer.
3. Mix the cornstarch with water in a small bowl and stir into the meat.
4. Add shredded carrots right before serving and heat through, allowing carrots to retain their crunch.
5. To serve, have guests scoop a tablespoon or two of meat onto an individual lettuce leaf and use the lettuce like a tortilla to hold the meat.
6. If desired, dip the lettuce rolls in Sweet Chili Dipping Sauce, pg. 71.

NUTRITIONAL STATS Servings 6, Serving size 251 g, Calories 190, Calories from fat 45, Fat 5 g, Saturated fat 1.5 g, Cholesterol 60 mg, Sodium 320 mg, Carbohydrate 9 g, Fiber 2 g, Protein 24 g

Ground Turkey Wrapped in Lettuce

1 T canola oil
1 medium onion, minced
1 jalapeno pepper, minced
1 green pepper, minced
1 can water chestnuts, drained and minced
1 clove garlic, minced
1 t turmeric
1 t coriander
1 T fresh ginger, minced or 1 t powdered
1½ lbs ground turkey
½ cup white wine
1 T fish sauce
1 cup shredded carrots
½ cup water
1 T cornstarch
1-2 bunches Boston, Bibb or red lettuce leaves

1. Place the oil in a frying pan over medium heat.
2. Add the onion, peppers, water chestnuts, garlic, turmeric, coriander and ginger. Sauté until vegetables are soft.
3. Add the turkey and cook until turkey is cooked through, stirring occasionally.
4. Reduce the heat to low; add the fish sauce and wine. Cover and cook for an additional 15 minutes. Add more water if necessary. The meat should be slightly moist.
5. Mix the cornstarch and water together and pour over the meat mixture. Cook over medium heat until meat mixture is slightly thickened, about 5 minutes more. Add the carrots and heat until carrots are hot but still retain their crunch. Serve wrapped in lettuce.

NUTRITIONAL STATS Servings 6, Serving size 297 g, Calories 210, Calories from fat 40, Fat 4 g, Saturated fat 0 g, Cholesterol 45 mg, Sodium 550 mg, Carbohydrate 13 g, Fiber 4 g, Protein 30 g

Sweet Chili Dipping Sauce

2 T canola oil
1 red pepper, minced
1 shallot, minced
2 T minced ginger
1 jalapeno pepper, minced
1 T minced lemongrass (optional)
1 lime, juiced
2 T honey
½ t salt

1. Put the oil in a small sauté pan and cook the red pepper, shallot, ginger, lemongrass and pepper until soft.
2. Deglaze with the lime juice.
3. Add the honey and salt and cook while stirring until honey is well blended.

NUTRITIONAL STATS Servings 8, Serving size 39 g, Calories 60, Calories from fat 30, Fat 3.5 g, Saturated fat 0 g, Cholesterol 0 mg, Sodium 150 mg, Carbohydrate 7 g, Fiber 0 g, Protein 0 g

Hungarian Goulash

1 large onion, chopped
1 T canola oil
1 lb stew meat
1 28-oz can unsalted diced tomatoes, including juice
2 T paprika
1 t pepper
2 carrots cut in 1-inch diagonal slices
8 small red potatoes, washed leaving skins on

1. In a Dutch oven over medium heat, sauté the onions in the oil until the onion is limp and mushy, stirring occasionally. This takes about 20 minutes. Watch carefully so the onions do not burn.
2. Add the meat, tomatoes and their juice, paprika, and pepper.
3. Bring the mixture to a boil, then cover and bake in the oven at 350º for 2 hours.
4. Add the carrots and potatoes, recover and continue baking for another hour or until carrots and potatoes are soft and meat is tender.

NUTRITIONAL STATS Servings 4, Serving size 433 g, Calories 350, Calories from fat 100, Fat 12 g, Saturated fat 3 g, Cholesterol 70 mg, Sodium 160 mg, Carbohydrate 34 g, Fiber 7 g, Protein 26 g

The Very Best Slow Oven-Roasted Pork

We like pork. Son Josh calls pork the best meat for college students because it is easy to prepare and reasonably priced. The pork in grocery stores today is leaner than what was available even a few years ago. But, while many cuts are low in fat, it means they are drier and require cooking techniques that retain moisture.

3 lbs boneless pork loin
2 T olive oil
2 T white wine
2 t freshly ground pepper
2 t salt
1 T powdered rosemary or 2 T fresh rosemary
2 t powdered sage
2 t powdered fennel
2 cloves garlic, minced

1. Preheat oven to 300º.
2. With a sharp knife, pierce the pork roast approximately 1-inch deep and ½-inch wide in about six places.
3. In a small bowl, combine the oil, wine, pepper, salt, rosemary, sage, fennel and garlic into a paste.
4. Rub the paste over the roast, filling the slits with the paste.
5. Place the roast on a baking pan and lightly cover with foil.
6. Bake for 3 hours, remove the foil and bake an additional 20 minutes. Baste with meat drippings while cooking.
7. Drizzle any pan drippings over the roast before serving.

NUTRITIONAL STATS Servings 10, Serving size 111 g, Calories 290, Calories from fat 160, Fat 18 g, Saturated fat 6 g, Cholesterol 85 mg, Sodium 530 mg, Carbohydrate 1 g, Fiber 0 g, Protein 28 g

Maple Chili Roasted Pork

This dish is quick, easy and amazingly good. The carrots are exceptional and the dish smells wonderful while roasting. If your family does not like carrots, arrange four cups of cleaned spinach around the meat during the last 10 minutes of baking. Serve the meat surrounded by the spinach and pour any pan juices over both.

1 pork tenderloin, about 1 lb
½ T canola oil
3 strips of bacon, thin cut
3 T pure maple syrup
2 t chipotle chili powder if available, or regular chili powder
2 t freshly ground black pepper
1 lb carrots, cut in sticks

1. Preheat the oven to 400°.
2. Lightly oil the bottom of a 9 x 13 inch baking pan with 1 teaspoon of oil or spray with cooking spray. Place the tenderloin in the baking pan.
3. In a small bowl, combine the maple syrup, 1½ teaspoons chipotle chili powder, salt and pepper. Spread this mixture evenly on the roast.
4. Starting at one end of the pork tenderloin, wrap the bacon strips around the tenderloin, one strip at a time from one end to the other.
5. Surround the roast with the carrot sticks. Mix remaining oil with remaining chipotle chili powder and drizzle over the carrots.
6. Bake uncovered for 45 minutes or until a meat thermometer reads 170°.

NUTRITIONAL STATS Servings 4, Serving size 263 g, Calories 350, Calories from fat 140, Fat 16 g, Saturated fat 5 g, Cholesterol 85 mg, Sodium 260 mg, Carbohydrate 24 g, Fiber 4 g, Protein 27 g

Easy Kraut and Pork Chops

1 T canola oil
4 pork chops, boneless preferred
1 large red onion, thinly sliced
1 can Bavarian sauerkraut

1. Place the oil in a frying pan over medium heat.
2. Add the onions and sauté for 5 minutes over medium heat until the onions are soft.
3. Push the onions to the side of the pan and add the pork chops and lightly brown.
4. Pour the sauerkraut over the meat, cover, and simmer for an hour or until pork is tender.

NUTRITIONAL STATS Servings 4, Serving size 217 g, Calories 250, Calories from fat 110, Fat 12 g, Saturated fat 3.5 g, Cholesterol 55 mg, Sodium 730 mg, Carbohydrate 19 g, Fiber 1 g, Protein 16 g

What is Bavarian sauerkraut?

IFC TIP

Bavarian kraut is a little more sweet and sour than regular sauerkraut and has caraway seeds. Even people who do not like sauerkraut often like this kind of kraut. If you cannot find it in your grocery, here is a simple way to *make your own:* Add two tablespoons of brown sugar and one tablespoon of caraway seed to regular sauerkraut.

Main Courses and Memorable Sauces

When I think about what makes many meals from good restaurants memorable, often what stands out is a particularly flavorful sauce. For food-lovers with multiple food intolerances, creating sauces that add interest to a dish is a challenge. The next two recipes include excellent and unusual sauces made from fruits or vegetables. These memorable sauces make them ideal choices for serving guests or as the centerpiece of a special meal.

Tomato Curry Pork Chops

6 center-cut pork chops, about 1-inch thick
1 t pepper
2 T canola oil
1 large onion, chopped
1 large red pepper, cut into thin slices
2 large cloves garlic, minced
1 T fresh basil, chopped
1 T curry powder
1 t chili powder
1 T fresh parsley, chopped
1 28-oz can diced low-sodium tomatoes, including juice
2 cups low-sodium GF stock
½ cup dry white wine
2 medium carrots, peeled and chopped into ½-inch pieces

1. Season the pork chops with pepper.
2. Heat the oil in a large, heavy skillet over medium heat. Add the pork and sauté until browned, about 3 minutes per side. Remove pork to drain on paper towels.
3. Add onion, pepper, and garlic to skillet and cook, stirring until vegetables are softened slightly, 4 to 5 minutes.
4. Add the basil, curry powder, chili powder, ½ tablespoon of parsley, and the tomatoes with their juice, stock and wine. Stir to combine.

5. Return pork to the skillet. Simmer, covered for 1 hour.
6. Add the chopped carrots and simmer another 20 to 30 minutes until the carrots and the meat are tender.
7. Remove the lid and simmer another 10 to 15 minutes until liquids are reduced to a slightly thick, sauce-like consistency.
8. To serve, arrange pork on serving platter and spoon the sauce over the meat. Sprinkle with remaining parsley. Serve with rice, quinoa or small red boiled potatoes.

NUTRITIONAL STATS Servings 6, Serving size 393 g, Calories 340, Calories from fat 150, Fat 17 g, Saturated fat 4.5 g, Cholesterol 70 mg, Sodium 230 mg, Carbohydrate 15 g, Fiber 3 g, Protein 28 g

Apple Braised Pork

4 thick pork chops, trimmed of fat
1 T olive oil
3 big Granny Smith apples, peeled, cored and chopped
1 medium red onion, thinly sliced
⅔ cup red wine
1 T paprika
½ t salt
1 t ground pepper

1. In an oven-safe skillet, sauté the pork over medium heat until lightly brown. Remove the pork to drain on paper towels.
2. Add the onions and cook until they are soft, about 5 minutes.
3. When the onions are soft, add the apples and wine and cook until soft, about 10 minutes.
4. While the onions and apples are cooking, preheat the oven to 350°.
5. Put the pork chops back into the skillet and cover. Place it in the oven and cook for 1 hour. Check during cooking and mash-up the apples and onions. While checking the dish, add extra water if needed, half a cup at a time. The apples and onions make a thick sauce to serve with the meat.
6. To serve, spoon the sauce over the chops. This dish is good with rice or red potatoes.

NUTRITIONAL STATS Servings 4, Serving size 261 g, Calories 280, Calories from fat 90, Fat 10 g, Saturated fat 2.5 g, Cholesterol 60 mg, Sodium 340 mg, Carbohydrate 19 g, Fiber 3 g, Protein 23 g

Chicken and Broccoli

FASTER THAN TAKE-OUT

This dish cooks quickly. Do the slicing and dicing in advance so the vegetables stay crisp and to shorten the time between preparing the dish and getting it to the table to feed hungry family members.

3 T oil
1 medium onion, sliced vertically
2 T fresh ginger, minced
2 cloves garlic, minced
1 jalapeno pepper, chopped
3 summer squash, peeled and sliced
2 c broccoli
2 T cornstarch
1 egg
1½ lbs boneless skinless chicken breast cut in bite-size chunks
¾ cup low-sodium GF broth
1 T fish sauce
1 T brown sugar
1 T cornstarch

1. Chop the onion, ginger, garlic and jalapeno pepper. Slice the squash in thin slices and separate the broccoli into small flowers.
2. Heat the oil in an electric frying pan set at 350° or in a large frying pan over medium-high heat.
3. Add the onion slices, ginger, garlic, jalapeno pepper and stir-fry for 2 to 3 minutes.
4. Whisk the cornstarch and egg together.
5. Pour the batter over the chicken chunks and stir to coat the chicken completely.
6. Add the chicken to the pan and fry until the chicken is lightly browned and almost cooked through, about 5 to 7 minutes.
7. Add the squash and broccoli and stir-fry for 3 to 5 minutes more.
8. Mix the broth, fish sauce, brown sugar and cornstarch together.
9. Pour the mixture over the chicken and vegetables and simmer until the chicken is completely cooked and the sauce is thick.
10. Serve with rice or rice noodles.

NUTRITIONAL STATS Servings 6, Serving size 280 g, Calories 260, Calories from fat 100, Fat 11 g, Saturated fat 1.5 g, Cholesterol 100 mg, Sodium 320 mg, Carbohydrate 14 g, Fiber 2 g, Protein 27 g

Fish Dishes

Fish and seafood are easy and quick to prepare. Yet many cooks—especially novice cooks—avoid preparing dishes based on seafood because they seem difficult. I hope the simple and simply delicious recipes featured here will change some minds. Although some fresh seafood is expensive, it is an economical food because there is so little waste. Frozen fish is a good option for some varieties of seafood, but make sure the fish thaws thoroughly before cooking. Pat dry with paper towel, removing excess moisture. When using individually frozen fillets, avoid brands dusted with flour before freezing.

Easy Baked Fish  FASTER THAN TAKE-OUT

1 lb. white fish, like cod or tilapia in individual fillets or cut in serving-size pieces
2 T olive oil
½ t salt
2 t freshly ground pepper
2 t lemon or lime zest
2 t paprika
1 lemon or 1 lime cut in wedges

1. Preheat the oven to 400°.
2. Lightly oil a baking pan with ½ tablespoon of oil or spray with cooking spray.
3. Combine the remaining oil with the salt, pepper, zest and paprika. Gently rub the seasoning mixture and oil over the top of the fish.
4. Bake for about 15 minutes or until fish is cooked through. Serve with lemon or lime wedges and Pesto Sauce, pg. 81.

NUTRITIONAL STATS Servings 4, Serving size 102 g, Calories 160, Calories from fat 70, Fat 8 g, Saturated fat 1 g, Cholesterol 45 mg, Sodium 350 mg, Carbohydrate 2 g, Fiber 1 g, Protein 18 g

Sweet-Spicy Glazed Salmon

FASTER THAN TAKE-OUT

3 T dark brown sugar
1 T fish sauce
4 t GF mustard
1 t unseasoned rice vinegar
4 salmon fillets about 6 ounces each
½ T olive oil
½ t salt
1 t freshly ground pepper

1. Preheat the oven to 425°.
2. Combine the brown sugar, fish sauce, mustard and vinegar in a small sauce pan and bring to boil to make the glaze. Remove from heat.
3. Place the fish on a foil-lined jelly roll pan lightly coated with olive oil. Season fish with salt and pepper and bake for 12 minutes. Remove the fish from the oven and preheat the broiler.
4. Brush the glaze over the fish and broil 3 inches from heat for 3 minutes, or until fish flakes easily when tested with a fork.

NUTRITIONAL STATS Servings 4, Serving size 174 g, Calories 330, Calories from fat 130, Fat 14 g, Saturated fat 2 g, Cholesterol 105 mg, Sodium 790 mg, Carbohydrate 10 g, Fiber 0 g, Protein 39 g

Super Fast Mediterranean Fish

FASTER THAN TAKE-OUT

1 lb cod or other white fish
2 T olive oil
1 clove garlic, minced
1 small onion cut in rings
1 tomato, sliced in thin slices
½ lb fresh green beans, tips removed
¼ cup dry white wine
1 lemon
¼ cup pitted black olives

1. Heat the olive oil and 1 clove of minced garlic over medium-high heat.
2. Add fish, skin side down. Cook 5 minutes until brown.
3. Flip over and cook for 3 minutes.
4. Place the onions, tomato slices, green beans on fish.
5. Add ¼ cup of wine and the juice of the lemon. Leave one of the lemon halves in the pan and cover.
6. Cook for 5 to 8 more minutes until the vegetables are cooked, the green beans remaining crisp.
7. Remove the cover for the last couple of minutes to thicken sauce, if necessary. Sprinkle with the olives.

NUTRITIONAL STATS Servings 4, Serving size 235 g, Calories 210, Calories from fat 80, Fat 9 g, Saturated fat 1 g, Cholesterol 45 mg, Sodium 140 mg, Carbohydrate 10 g, Fiber 3 g, Protein 19 g

When It Has to Be Fried Fish

The Friday night fish fry is a long-standing Wisconsin tradition. It seems like nearly every restaurant in the state, every corner bar that serves food, many church basements and VFW halls fire up the fry machines on Friday night. The smell of batter-fried fish is in the air. As a gluten intolerant, fish fries like these belong to a previous life. This recipe feeds my nostalgic craving for a little something fried.

1 pound white fish, cut in serving-size pieces, cod works well, rinsed and patted dry on paper towels
1 cup corn meal
½ t salt
2 t freshly ground pepper
2 t paprika
1 t cayenne pepper
½ cup rice milk or other milk substitute
½ cup canola oil

1. Place the milk substitute in a cereal bowl.
2. Mix the corn meal and seasonings in another bowl.
3. Dip the fish in the milk substitute and then in the seasoned corn meal.
4. Heat the oil in a frying pan over medium-high heat. Oil is ready when a drop of water sizzles. Do not let the oil reach the smoking stage.
5. Place the breaded fish in the frying pan and cook for 5 to 7 minutes on one side.
6. Turn the fish and cook another 5 to 7 minutes on the other side until the fish is cooked through and corn meal is lightly browned.

NUTRITIONAL STATS Servings 4, Serving size 208 g, Calories 480, Calories from fat 270, Fat 30 g, Saturated fat 2 g, Cholesterol 50 mg, Sodium 370 mg, Carbohydrate 28 g, Fiber 6 g, Protein 23 g

Shrimp with Excellent Almond Pepper Sauce

Unlike many families, we never had one standard menu for our main meal at Christmas. Over the years, we tried many interesting and tasty meals, but nothing was better than the excellent shrimp dish that Heather and Stephen served us as we all gathered for the first time at their home in Texas. This dish has a substantial almond-based sauce you can serve with the rice alone for the vegetarians at your holiday table. Make the sauce ahead to keep actual preparation time short.

4-8 cloves garlic, unpeeled
2 jalapeno peppers, cut in half, core removed
1 red pepper, cut in quarters, core removed
1 large tomato, halved
½ cup slivered almonds
¼ cup olive oil
2 T red wine vinegar
1 t salt
2 t freshly ground pepper
1½ lbs large shrimp, shelled and deveined
1 t ancho chili powder
¼ cup dry white wine

1. Preheat the oven to 350°.
2. Place the jalapenos peppers, red pepper, garlic and tomato halves on a baking pan and bake about 25 minutes or until the garlic is light brown and tender.
3. Put the almonds on a pie plate and bake for about 7 minutes or until light brown.
4. When these ingredients are cool, peel the garlic and blend the ingredients together in a food processor or hand blender. Slowly add 3 tablespoons of the olive oil, the vinegar and cayenne pepper. You can make ahead and refrigerate.
5. Place remaining oil in a frying pan and heat until warm over medium heat. Add salt, pepper and chili powder to the oil and stir until blended. Add the shrimp and cook 1 to 2 minutes on each side.
6. Pour the wine over the shrimp and cook 1 to 2 minutes more until the shrimp is pink and cooked through.
7. Remove the shrimp from pan, place on a serving dish.
8. Simmer the wine until it thickens, about 1 additional minute. Then pour the sauce over the shrimp. Serve with almond sauce and Spinach Rice.

NUTRITIONAL STATS Servings 6, Serving size 201 g, Calories 290, Calories from fat 150, Fat 16 g, Saturated fat 2 g, Cholesterol 170 mg, Sodium 360 mg, Carbohydrate 8 g, Fiber 2 g, Protein 26 g

Spinach Rice

1 T olive oil
1 cup basmati rice
3 cups raw spinach, washed and roughly chopped
2 cups water
½ t salt
1 T minced shallot or onion

1. Place the oil in a medium sauce pan over medium heat.
2. Add the shallot or onion and sauté until lightly browned.
3. Add the spinach and salt. Cook until the spinach wilts.
4. Add the rice and water. Bring to a boil.
5. Cover and reduce the heat to simmer for 15 minutes.
6. Remove from heat and let sit covered until rice is cooked and moisture is absorbed. Stir to distribute the spinach evenly before serving.

NUTRITIONAL STATS Servings 4, Serving size 103 g, Calories 130, Calories from fat 25, Fat 2.5 g, Saturated fat 0 g, Cholesterol 0 mg, Sodium 320 mg, Carbohydrate 25 g, Fiber 1 g, Protein 3 g

Pesto Sauce for Fish or Chicken

½ T cumin
1 medium white onion
Zest and juice of 2 limes
2 T fresh parsley or cilantro, chopped
1 T fresh mint, chopped
1 t sea salt
2 t ground pepper
2 T olive oil

1. Put the cumin, onion, lime juice and zest, parsley or cilantro, and mint in a blender or food processor.
2. Pulse ingredients together until well chopped, do not puree. Add olive oil and pulse until well blended.

NUTRITIONAL STATS Servings 10, Serving size 23 g, Calories 35, Calories from fat 25, Fat 3 g, Cholesterol 0 g, Sodium 120 mg, Carbohydrate 2 g, Fiber 0 g, Protein 0g

Rice Noodle Bowls

There are Asian restaurants springing up all over the country and a number of chains now serve noodle bowls—some of them gluten-free. Rice noodles and fish sauce make Asian-inspired noodle dishes an excellent choice in a GF, DF diet. Rice noodles come in a variety of widths, but we like the thin ones best. It is easy to prepare rice bowls, hot (as in spicy) or less hot according to family tastes. We like to throw in several dried hot chilies during cooking to ensure a little extra heat. Two versions of rice bowls follow. The Coconut Soup in the *Soups* chapter is similar.

Rice Bowl with Red Sauce

1 package thin rice noodles, usually 6.5 ounces
1 T oil
2 T fresh ginger, minced
2 T fresh cilantro, chopped plus some for garnish
1 small onion, sliced
½ cup GF ketchup
1 14.5-oz can diced low-sodium tomatoes including juice
2 cups GF low-sodium chicken broth
1 T fish sauce
⅓ cup lime juice
2 t cayenne or 3 or more dried hot red peppers
2 cups fresh bean sprouts or a 14-oz can, drained
3 spring onions, sliced
2 cups cooked chicken or shrimp
½ cup peanuts, divided
1 lime, sliced in four vertical sections

1. Prepare the rice noodles according package directions, usually by softening in hot water.
2. Place the oil in a wok or Dutch oven over medium heat.
3. Add the ginger, cilantro and onion, and sauté about 5 minutes or until the onion is limp.
4. In a small bowl, combine the ketchup, tomatoes, chicken broth, fish sauce and lime juice. Pour mixture in the wok or Dutch oven and stir to combine.
5. Add the cayenne or hot peppers.
6. Drain the noodles and add to the sauce.
7. Add the bean sprouts, spring onions and chicken or shrimp. Stir while cooking, 5 minutes or until all food is heated.
8. Stir in ¼ cup of peanuts. Place in four serving bowls; garnish with cilantro, ¼ cup of peanuts, serve with lime sections.

NUTRITIONAL STATS Servings 4, Serving size 524 g, Calories 550, Calories from fat 150, Fat 17 g, Saturated fat 2.5 g, Cholesterol 60 mg, Sodium 870 mg, Carbohydrate 64 g, Fiber 6 g, Protein 35 g

FASTER THAN TAKE-OUT

Ginger Rice Noodle Bowl
FASTER THAN TAKE-OUT

1 package thin rice noodles
2 T oil
2 cloves garlic
¼ cup thinly sliced ginger
1 small onion, thinly sliced
1 lb chicken breast, cut in bite-size chunks
2 cups GF low sodium chicken stock
1 cup water
1 T fish sauce
2 T lime juice
2 hot red peppers, more or less to taste
1 cup thinly sliced jicama
½ cup coarsely shredded carrots plus 2 T for garnish
1 red pepper cut in thin strips
4 green onions cut crosswise, reserving 2 T for garnish

1. Prepare the rice noodles according to package directions, usually by softening in hot water.
2. Put the oil in a wok or Dutch oven and heat over medium heat.
3. Add the garlic, ginger, onion and the chicken breast, cook until the chicken is lightly browned.
4. Add the stock, water, fish sauce, lime juice and peppers. Heat, stirring until very hot.
5. Add the jicama, carrots, spring onions, red pepper and well-drained rice noodles.
6. Cook and stir for 2 to 3 minutes more, leaving the vegetables crisp.
7. Garnish with carrot and onion slices.

NUTRITIONAL STATS Servings 4, Serving size 430 g, Calories 430, Calories from fat 90, Fat 10 g, Saturated fat 1.5 g, Cholesterol 65 mg, Sodium 490 mg, Carbohydrate 49 g, Fiber 4 g, Protein 30 g

No wok around?
IFC TIP

While a wok is a great pan to have for doing a stir-fry meal—or for steaming and braising—a large frying pan is a good substitute for preparing most dishes. An electric frying pan is another stand-in that works well.

Veggies

Fresh vegetables are an important part of our family meals and have been since the children were small. For many years, Allyn was an avid gardener, tending a garden plot at a neighborhood community garden site. He enjoyed gardening and meeting with friends and neighbors who belonged to this enthusiastic gardening community. Not everything grew, but at the end of every summer, we always looked forward to lots of fresh tomatoes and peppers, all the zucchini we could eat and even more to give away.

We are fortunate to live in a city that has great farmers' markets and opportunities for direct farmer-to-consumer vegetable buying through Community Supported Agriculture (CSA) programs. We no longer garden but because we are members of a CSA, we still get the pleasure of bringing home a basket full of locally grown fresh vegetables every week and planning how to use them in a variety of nutritious, delicious ways—especially the unfamiliar ones.

Vegetables provide nutrients and fiber to your diet. Many are low in carbohydrates, an added plus for people who count carbs. Whatever your source for fresh vegetables, make sure to wash everything thoroughly before cooking or serving raw.

MOLLY REMEMBERS: When we were little, Dad liked to garden at the community garden. Because it was located near the swimming pool in our town, we kids would go to the garden with Dad but always end up at the swimming pool while he worked in the garden.

When Gregg and I first got married, we were living in Madison and thought we would like to have our own garden. We got a plot at the community garden where Dad had his plot. Unfortunately, Gregg and I were not the best garden weeders and our plot was overgrown in no time. Dad tried not to nag us about our unsightly plot and we never saw him work in it. But we did notice, at one point, the garden miraculously began to look much less unsightly and learned that Dad was disappearing from home in the evenings to work unnoticed in our plot.

Molly's Veggie Frittata

FASTER THAN TAKE-OUT

MOLLY RECALLS: Easter weekend 2003 was the first time Gregg's parents and my parents met. Gregg's parents, who live in Houston, Texas, came to Wisconsin to find a location for our wedding rehearsal dinner and to see what it is like in the north. The weekend was a success. I thought an excellent conclusion to the parent summit was to host an Easter Brunch at my apartment. Veggie Frittata is a great dish because it satisfies both intolerant and tolerant eaters in the family, and was so simple to make, I could spend most of my time talking instead of cooking. This version uses my favorite vegetables but feel free to experiment with your own unique mixture of vegetables. The Frittata also makes a good quick emergency supper dish.

1 T olive oil
9 eggs or GF egg substitute, or 5 eggs and 4 whites
¼ cup milk substitute
2 T fresh basil, chopped
2 Roma tomatoes, diced
3 green onions, sliced
4 cloves garlic, minced
2 cups mushrooms, sliced
2 cups fresh spinach
1 t salt
1 t pepper

1. Preheat the oven to 350°.
2. Place the eggs and milk substitute in a large bowl. Add 1½ tablespoons basil, salt and pepper, and scramble with a fork or whisk. Set aside.
3. Over medium heat, sauté the garlic in the olive oil in a large ovenproof frying pan.
4. Add the mushrooms and green onions and cook for about 5 minutes, until most of the mushroom juice evaporates.
5. Add the tomatoes and spinach and cook until spinach wilts, another minute or two.
6. Spread the veggies evenly over the bottom of the frying pan and carefully pour the egg mixture over the top. Continue cooking until eggs begin to get firm.
7. Place pan in the oven and bake for 12-15 minutes.
8. Garnish with remaining basil.

NUTRITIONAL STATS Servings 6, Serving size 166 g, Calories 160, Calories from fat 90, Fat 10 g, Saturated fat 2.5 g, Cholesterol 315 mg, Sodium 320 mg, Carbohydrate 6 g, Fiber 1 g, Protein 11 g

Ratatouille

We started eating ratatouille one summer as a way to deal with zucchini overload. It's an excellent summer dish when the vegetables come straight from the garden. If you do not have a garden, visit a local farmers' market where picking out fresh summer vegetables is a memorable family outing.

¼ cup olive oil
2 cloves garlic, minced
1 medium onion, sliced
1 green pepper, cut into strips
3 medium zucchini, peeled and cut into ¼-inch slices
1 medium young eggplant, pared, peeled and cut into ½-1-inch cubes
1 T fresh basil, chopped
1 t oregano
1 t salt
1 t freshly ground pepper
3 tomatoes, peeled and cut into wedges
½ cup ripe olives

1. Heat the oil over medium heat in a large skillet.
2. Add garlic, onion and green pepper; cook until onion is tender.
3. Add the zucchini, eggplant, basil, oregano, salt and pepper to the cooking vegetables.
4. Cover and cook over medium heat for 15 minutes, stirring occasionally.
5. Add the tomatoes and the olives.
6. Cover and cook 5 to 10 minutes longer.

Serving note: If you like the veggies somewhat crisp, the dish is ready to serve at this point. It is even better if you bake it in the oven, covered, at 300° for another hour or two. The flavor gets better as the dish bakes. Or refrigerate the ratatouille and serve later, warm or cold. Add grated cheese at serving for the dairy tolerant. Leftovers make a good filling for omelets or GF tortillas.

NUTRITIONAL STATS Servings 8, Serving size 180 g, Calories 120, Calories from fat 80, Fat 9 g, Saturated fat 1 g, Cholesterol 0 mg, Sodium 420 mg, Carbohydrate 10 g, Fiber 4 g, Protein 2 g

Gourmet Veggie Pasta

8 oz dry GF pasta
Enough water to cook pasta according to package directions
¼ cup olive oil
1-2 shallots
1 red pepper, thinly sliced
1 cup canned artichokes, cut in bite-size pieces and well drained
6 cups spinach, washed and thick stems removed
½ cup walnuts
3 plum tomatoes, sliced.
½ cup balsamic vinegar
1 t black pepper
½ t nutmeg

1. Heat the water in a large pan to boiling. Add the GF pasta and boil until soft. GF pasta usually takes about 15 minutes to cook, but follow package directions. While the pasta cooks, prepare the sauce.
2. Place the oil in a large frying pan over medium heat. Add the walnuts and brown lightly. Remove and set aside.
3. Add shallots, red pepper and artichokes to the frying pan. Sauté until shallots are soft, about 5 minutes.
4. Add the spinach, tomatoes and balsamic vinegar, and cook until spinach is wilted, about 3 to 5 more minutes.
5. Stir in pepper and nutmeg. Simmer over low heat until pasta is cooked. Add walnuts to the sauce right before serving.
6. Drain the pasta and place in a large bowl or individual serving dishes. Pour vegetable mixture over pasta.

NUTRITIONAL STATS Servings 4, Serving size 352 g, Calories 530, Calories from fat 230, Fat 25 g, Saturated fat 3 g, Cholesterol 0 g, Sodium 720 mg, Carbohydrate 71 g, Fiber 14 g, Protein 12 g

Spinach Pesto for Pasta  FASTER THAN TAKE-OUT

This is another good veggie sauce for pasta. If you tolerate aged Parmesan cheese or Romano cheese add half a cup of grated cheese to the pesto. We were pleased to find the pesto is good even without the cheese.

1 cup spinach leaves, packed
¼ cup fresh parsley
¼ cup fresh basil
½ cup pine nuts or ½ cup walnuts
½ cup olive oil
2 t salt
2 t freshly ground pepper

1. Place the spinach, parsley, basil and nuts in a food processor or blender and pulse.
2. Stream in the olive oil and blend until well blended and relatively smooth. Add another tablespoon of oil if needed.
3. To serve, toss with prepared hot pasta.

NUTRITIONAL STATS Servings 4, Serving size 58 g, Calories 360, Calories from fat 340, Fat 38 g, Saturated fat 5 g, Cholesterol 0 mg, Sodium 590 mg, Carbohydrate 4 g, Dietary fiber 2 g, Protein 3 g

Note: Nutritional stats do not include the pasta.

Mashed Cauliflower

1 head of cauliflower
2 cloves of garlic, crushed
¼ cup GF plain milk substitute
¼ cup olive oil
½ t salt
1 t pepper

1. Steam cauliflower in about two inches of water over medium heat until soft to the touch but not too mushy.
2. Drain the cauliflower well.
3. Mash the cauliflower with garlic, salt, pepper, milk substitute and olive oil. Cauliflower should be the consistency of mashed potatoes.

NUTRITIONAL STATS Servings 4, Serving size 176 g, Calories 170, Calories from fat 130, Fat 14 g, Saturated fat 2 g, Cholesterol 0 mg, Sodium 340 mg, Carbohydrate 9 g, Fiber 4 g, Protein 3 g

Fried Rice with Fruits and Vegetables

2 cups cooked long-grain rice
2 T canola oil
1 small red onion, halved and sliced thinly
2 shallots, thinly sliced, or two gloves garlic, minced
1 T grated fresh ginger
½ cup chopped tomatoes
½ 8-oz can of crushed pineapple, well drained
2 T fish sauce
3 green onions, sliced diagonally

1. Cook rice according to package directions or use leftover rice.
2. While rice is cooking, slice and chop the remaining ingredients.
3. Place the oil in the bottom of a wok over medium heat. The oil should be hot but not smoking.
4. Add the onions and shallots or garlic and cook until tender.
5. Add ginger and cook for another minute.
6. Add the cooked rice and fry for 2 to 3 minutes over high heat.
7. Add the tomatoes and pineapple and cook 2 to 3 minutes more.
8. Add the fish sauce and green onions, toss and cook until the rice is heated thorough. Watch carefully to avoid burning rice.

NUTRITIONAL STATS Servings 4, Serving size 219 g, Calories 220, Calories from fat 70, Fat 7 g, Saturated fat .5 g, Cholesterol 0 g, Sodium 700 mg, Carbohydrate 36 g, Fiber 2 g, Protein 4 g

Roasted Asparagus

Roasting vegetables creates a unique flavor. We started out roasting winter root vegetables, moved on to asparagus and then added cauliflower and Brussels sprouts to the list as vegetables that taste good roasted. For this recipe, feel free to substitute either one for the asparagus.

1½ lbs of fresh asparagus, washed, woody ends removed
2 T olive oil
Juice of half a lemon
½ t salt
1 t pepper

1. Preheat the oven to 400°.
2. Lightly oil a jelly roll pan with ½ tablespoon of the oil.
3. Place the asparagus on the pan and drizzle remaining oil over the top; sprinkle with salt and pepper.
4. Roast 10 minutes.
5. Remove the asparagus from the oven and squeeze the lemon juice over it while hot. Serve hot, warm or cold.

NUTRITIONAL STATS Servings 6, Serving size 121 g, Calories 70, Calories from fat 45, Fat 5 g, Saturated fat .5 g, Cholesterol 0 mg, Sodium 200 mg, Carbohydrate 5 g, Dietary fiber 2 g, Protein 3 g

Red Cabbage

1 T oil
1 medium red onion, sliced in thin slices
4 cups shredded red cabbage
1 large apple, chopped
½ cup raisins
½ cup red wine vinegar
3 T brown sugar
1 t nutmeg
1 t salt
1 t pepper

1. In a large ovenproof pan, sauté the onion in the oil over low heat until the onion is mushy.
2. Add the rest of the ingredients, stir well to combine and sauté until the cabbage is wilted.
3. Cover the pan and bake in the oven at 325° for 2 hours, checking occasionally. Add water, a few tablespoons at a time, if needed. Serve warm.

NUTRITIONAL STATS Servings 6, Serving size 155 g, Calories 140, Calories from fat 25, Fat 2.5 g, Saturated fat 0 g, Cholesterol 0 mg, Sodium 210 mg, Carbohydrate 31 g, Fiber 3 g, Protein 2 g

Faux Hash Browns

1 spaghetti squash
3 T olive oil
½ medium onion, chopped
1 clove garlic, minced
1 jalapeno pepper, seeded and chopped
2 t chili powder
½ t salt
1 t freshly ground pepper

1. Cut the squash in half, remove the seeds and cover with plastic wrap. Place in a microwave-safe shallow baking pan with half-inch of water in the bottom.
2. Microwave for about 8 minutes. Microwaves vary so additional time may be necessary. Cook until squash is soft. Once the squash is cooked, drain well.
3. Heat the oil in a frying pan over medium heat.
4. Add the garlic and onion and cook for about 2 minutes.
5. Add squash, jalapeno pepper, chili powder, salt and pepper.
6. Fry until crisp and squash starts to look like hash browns.

NUTRITIONAL STATS Servings 4, Serving size 223 g, Calories 170, Calories from fat 100, Fat 12 g, Saturated fat 1 g, Cholesterol 0 mg, Sodium 320 mg, Carbohydrate 16 g, Fiber 2 g, Protein 2 g

Oven Fries

Gluten intolerants know that unless restaurants operate fryers dedicated only to French fries, the risk of cross contamination makes ordering fries when eating out off limits. This tasty, lower-fat version is another good argument for home cooking and will make you forget why you minded not eating restaurant French fries.

4 good-size potatoes, scrubbed clean, skins can be left on
2 T canola oil
½ t kosher salt
1 t pepper

1. Preheat the oven to 400°.
2. Spread the oil evenly on a jelly roll pan.
3. Cut the potatoes lengthwise so they look like French fries.
4. Place the potatoes in a single layer on the pan. Salt and pepper the potatoes and bake for 45 minutes or until they are crispy and brown. Stir occasionally.

NUTRITIONAL STATS Servings 4, Serving size 307 g, Calories 340, Calories from fat 70, Fat 7 g, Saturated fat .5 g, Cholesterol 0 mg, Sodium 320 mg, Carbohydrate 64 g, Dietary fiber 7 g, Protein 8 g

Sweet Potatoes

The sweet potato is a wonderful vegetable with a bad reputation because it is too often lost in a mixture of marshmallows and brown sugar. In fact, sweet potatoes are a tasty, healthy alternative to regular potatoes, and a good source of fiber that is easy to incorporate into any diet. We like them baked in their skins, like a baked potato, but also enjoy these other variations on a sweet-potato theme.

Rosemary Baked Sweet Potatoes

This dish is amazingly good and easy to prepare. An excellent option for an Easter buffet or dinner anytime.

4 medium sweet potatoes, peeled and cut in 1-inch chunks
3 T olive oil
2 t powdered rosemary, or 2 T fresh rosemary, minced
1 clove garlic, minced
½ t salt
1 t pepper

1. Preheat the oven to 375°.
2. Spread 1 tablespoon of the olive oil over the bottom of a 9 X 13 inch pan.
3. Place the sweet potato chunks in the pan.
4. Mix the rosemary, garlic, salt and pepper with the remaining oil and drizzle over the potatoes.
5. Bake for about 1 hour until chunks are soft.

NUTRITIONAL STATS Servings 6, Serving size 96 g, Calories 140, Calories from fat 60, Fat 7 g, Saturated fat 1 g, Cholesterol 0 mg, Sodium 240 mg, Carbohydrate 18 g, Fiber 3 g, Protein 2 g

Sort-of-Sweet Baked Sweet Potatoes

If you think sweet potatoes must be sweet, here is a way to prepare them that is sweet but not too sweet.

3 medium sweet potatoes
1 14-oz can pineapple chunks sweetened in its own juice, reserving juice
½ cup orange juice
2 T olive oil
½ t salt
1 t pepper

1. Preheat the oven to 375°.
2. Lightly rub one tablespoon of olive oil over the bottom of a 13 X 9 inch baking pan.
3. Peel the sweet potatoes and cut in 1-inch thick slices.
4. Place the sweet potatoes on the bottom of the baking pan.
5. Drain the pineapple juice from the pineapple chunks, reserving juice. Place the drained pineapple chunks in the baking pan with the sweet potatoes.
6. Mix a half cup of the drained pineapple juice with the orange juice and remaining oil. Drizzle the juice mixture over the top of the potatoes.
7. Sprinkle the salt and pepper over the potatoes.
8. Bake, uncovered for 45 minutes to an hour until the sweet potatoes are soft.

NUTRITIONAL STATS Servings 6, Serving size 96 g, Calories 140, Calories from fat 60, Fat 7 g, Saturated fat 1 g, Cholesterol 0 mg, Sodium 240 mg, Carbohydrate 18 g, Fiber 3 g, Protein 2 g

Sautéed Spinach

1 bag cleaned, washed and dried spinach, thick stems removed
2 T olive oil
2 cloves garlic, minced
1 small onion, chopped or 1 shallot, chopped
½ t salt
1 t pepper

1. Heat the oil in a frying pan over medium heat. When the oil is warm, add the garlic and onion and sauté until lightly browned.
2. Add the spinach, salt and pepper, and sauté until soft and cooked, 3 to 5 minutes.
3. Serve immediately.

NUTRITIONAL STATS Servings 4, Serving size 112 g, Calories 110, Calories from fat 60, Fat 7 g, Saturated fat 1 g, Cholesterol 0 mg, Sodium 430 mg, Carbohydrate 11 g, Dietary fiber 4 g, Protein 2 g

Grilled Corn on the Cob

4 ears of corn, silk removed but retaining the husks

1. Remove the outer layer of husk and remove the corn silk. Close the remaining husks over the ear and place the corn in a large bowl of water. Let the corn sit in the water for an hour or more so the husks are very wet.
2. Prepare the grill, either charcoal or gas. When the grill is hot, place the corn in the husks on the grill and cook for 15 to 20 minutes. The husks will dry out and begin to blacken. Turn the corn every 5 minutes. The corn is best when some of the kernels blacken. The smoky flavor makes the corn especially tasty.
3. Remove the husks and serve with salt, pepper and DF margarine at the table so everyone can flavor the corn according to their tastes.

NUTRITIONAL STATS Servings 4, Serving size 82 g, Calories 80, Calories from fat 15, Fat 1.5 g, Saturated fat .5 g, Cholesterol 0 mg, Sodium 5 mg, Carbohydrate 13 g, Fiber 4 g, Protein 3 g

Breads

Before I became food intolerant, I defined a good restaurant by the quality of its bread. Good bread was the one thing I missed the most as an intolerant and I became determined to find satisfying alternatives that allowed me to continue the tradition of having the scent of freshly baked bread in my kitchen.

Home-baked is best, of course. But there are more GF breads available commercially all the time. Bakeries and grocery stores in the moderate-size city where I live offer freshly baked GF products. Unless you live in a very small community, baking your own is not as important as it was just a few years ago and, at minimum, almost every grocery store carries gluten- and dairy-free corn tortillas.

I find there are fewer commercial sources for fresh-baked bread products that are both gluten- and dairy- free, but many stores carry frozen breads in this category. There are additional web sources where you can order bread products online. Despite having more options in the marketplace, I confess I still like the idea of pulling my own baked bread from the oven.

GF flour challenge

Working with GF flours is challenging. The taste is not the same as wheat flour, nor is the consistency. I use a mixture of flours that I developed after experimenting with many different flour combinations. When I first became gluten intolerant, I bought a bread machine and tried making my breads in that, but I was never really happy with the result. I went back to using my heavy-duty mixer and the regular mixer beater. This machine handles heavy batters easily, unlike a lightweight hand-held mixer.

You can buy one of the commercially available gluten-free, ready-to-use flour mixtures or make your own. Either way, one advantage of GF flours is they only need one rise and there is no kneading. This means you can prepare yeast breads quickly and easily.

GF flour mixture

When I first started baking with GF flours, I was concerned that they were short on fiber, protein and other nutrients. Since I try not to eat empty calories, I continue to experiment to find a combination of flours that provides reasonably good nutrition and makes a decent baked product. What follows is the basic combination of flours I use as my core flour. I measure portions of the flours together in a tub, then cover and shake the contents until well combined. I store the flour mix in the refrigerator.

For my basic GF flour mixture, I blend specific amounts of brown rice, sorghum and amaranth flours together. Amaranth has a distinctive flavor that makes it an acquired taste and it is more expensive than the other flours, but I find having it in the mix makes a better baked product. If the taste of the flour blend is in any way unpalatable, try adding spices to your batter. Honey or maple syrup used as sweeteners also help make a better-flavored product.

To make your own GF blend following my recipe, combine these flours and amounts in a storage container.

5 cups brown rice flour
3 cups sorghum flour
2 cups amaranth flour

Helpful yeast tip

I buy my dry yeast in 16-ounce bags, available in the baking section of most grocery stores, and store it in the refrigerator. It lasts a long time and is less expensive than individual packets of yeast. I use one tablespoon of yeast per loaf for most breads I bake.

Start with basics

Several recipes—like the one that begins this chapter—serve as the basis for most of my bread baking. I add different seasonings to create interesting flavors in breads and the other baked goods in my repertoire. Buckwheat flour, for example, is an ingredient that makes a great brown bread. Occasionally, I add tapioca flour or cornstarch to my dessert baking.

I like to use large silicone muffin pans to make sandwich buns from this basic recipe to use with hamburgers or other sandwich fillings. The recipe makes 12 buns and one small loaf baked in a 4 x 8 or similar-sized pan. Fill the muffin cups about one-third full. That gives them room to rise but still achieve the thickness of a bun. You also can bake a loaf in a standard-size bread pan.

Unless the place where you do your baking is very cool, this basic bread usually takes about 30 to 45 minutes to rise. Place the loaves in the oven when slightly less than doubled in height. Follow these baking times for bread in a 360° preheated oven:

Buns: 20 to 25 minutes
Small loaf: 25 to 30 minutes
Regular-size loaf: 60 to 70 minutes

Storing GF breads

All bread tastes best fresh from the oven. The same is true for GF breads, despite GF baking tips I see that recommend letting the bread cool completely before cutting or eating. I always eat some fresh from the oven as a special treat.

Even my husband Allyn, an avowed non-GF bread eater, enjoys sampling it then.

These breads freeze well. I usually freeze half of each batch as soon as it cools completely. I like to make individual "buns" that I store in a freezer bag in the freezer so it is easy to use them one or two at a time without thawing the entire bag. GF breads always taste better and hold their texture better when warm so, if I am eating at home, I toast the bread or bun. For sandwiches eaten away from home, warm in a microwave, if available, for about 30 seconds before eating.

MOLLY RECALLS: Winters in our family always meant the smell of warm bread. Great hearty breads like beer bread or cheese bread were my favorites. I associate them with brisk fall days, the Green Bay Packers and bad TV shows like "Kung Fu: The Legend Returns"—which Mom used to watch while making bread. GF bread doesn't have quite the same ring to it that beer and cheese bread do, but the smell of baking bread, no matter what kind, still makes me feel entirely at home in my mother's kitchen. And nothing beats warm bread on a winter day, especially served alongside a good hearty winter soup or chili.

Basic Bread

½ cup warm water
1 T dry yeast
3 cups GF flour mixture
1 t salt
2½ t xanthan gum
1 egg and 2 egg whites from medium eggs
1¼ cups warm water or milk substitute
2 T canola or light olive oil
1 t cider vinegar
2 T maple syrup or honey
2 T sesame seeds, flax meal or nut meal

1. Mix ½ cup warm water with yeast and set aside.
2. Place the GF flour, salt, xanthan gum in a large mixer bowl and stir until combined.
3. In a smaller bowl mix the eggs, 1¼ cups water or milk substitute, oil, vinegar and maple syrup, and add yeast mixture to it.
4. Using the mixer at a low speed, combine the wet and dry ingredients. Then beat for 3 to 4 minutes on high speed.
5. Stop the mixer after 2 minutes and add seeds, meal or additional seasonings. Blend for 30 seconds and continue beating at high speed for another minute or 2, until batter is soft and fluffy. The resulting batter is thicker than cake batter but not as thick as cookie dough. If it is too stiff, add more water, 1 tablespoon at a time.
6. Let rise in loaf pan 30 to 45 minutes, then bake in pre-heated 360° oven for 60 to 70 minutes, 20 to 25 minutes for buns.

NUTRITIONAL STATS Servings 16, Serving size 58 g, Calories 150, Calories from fat 35, Fat 3.5 g, Saturated fat 0 g, Cholesterol 15 mg, Sodium 160 mg, Carbohydrate 26 g, Fiber 2 g, Protein 4g

Spice up the basic bread

Because GF flours give breads a different taste than what I used to eat, I like to spice up my GF breads with seasonings. This creates products that taste more like the specialty breads you find in bakeries. Here are some ideas for enhancing the flavor of your bread. Feel free to experiment with your own favorites and if you tolerate it, a half-cup of grated cheese is an excellent addition. Add these seasonings near the end of the mixing and make sure to distribute them evenly.

2 T chives, 2 t freshly ground pepper & 1 t cayenne pepper, **or**
1 T dill & 2 T finely minced white onion or shallots, **or**
2 t dried oregano & 2 t dried basil

Brown Bread

This bread is similar to the Basic Bread recipe except I substitute buckwheat flour for some of the flour mixture. This is my favorite and the bread I bake most often.

½ cup warm water
1 T yeast
2½ cups GF flour
½ cup buckwheat flour
1 t salt
2½ t xanthan gum
1 egg and 2 egg whites from medium eggs
1¼ cups water or milk substitute
2 T canola or light olive oil
1 t cider vinegar
3 T mild molasses
2 T sesame seeds or nut meal

Prepare by following *Basic Bread* recipe, pg. 101.

Brown Bread Variations

To the other ingredients, add:
2 t cinnamon
½ cup finely chopped walnuts
½ cup raisins

or

Substitute 1¼ cups orange juice for the water and add:
1 T orange zest
2 T toasted sunflower seeds

NUTRITIONAL STATS Servings 16, Serving size 42 g, Calories 140, Calories from fat 30, Fat 3.5 g, Saturated fat 0 g, Cholesterol 15 mg, Sodium 160 mg, Carbohydrate 24 g, Fiber 2 g, Protein 4 g

Corn Bread

1 cup GF flour mix
1 cup corn meal
1½ t xanthan gum
1 T GF baking powder
2 T sugar
2 medium eggs
1 cup milk substitute
3 T canola oil
1 t salt

1. Preheat the oven to 400°.
2. Place all ingredients in a bowl and mix by hand or with a mixer for 3 to 4 minutes.
3. Pour the batter into a greased 8-inch square pan and bake for about 25 minutes until the bread is lightly browned and springs back when lightly touched.

Optional added ingredients:
If you like your corn bread on the bold side, add any of the following:

1 jalapeno pepper, finely minced
1 red pepper, finely chopped
1 cup corn kernels, out of the can and drained, or kernels sliced from leftover corn-on-the-cob. Especially good with corn-on-the-cob roasted on the grill.

NUTRITIONAL STATS Servings 9, Serving size 79 g, Calories 180, Calories from fat 60, Fat 7 g, Saturated fat .5 g, Cholesterol 45 mg, Sodium 470 mg, Carbohydrate 27 g, Dietary fiber 4 g, Protein 4 g

IFC TIP: Know your milk substitutes

There are many choices on the list of substitutes for milk in the diets of people who learn for the first time they are dairy intolerant—and that list often begins with soy milk. That was my first choice but slowly I became less tolerant of soy milk and moved on to rice milk and nut milks. Because of my gluten intolerance, I also look for milk substitutes labeled gluten-free. Any of these products work well in dairy-free cooking. I recommend reserving the vanilla-flavored versions for use in puddings or desserts, as they tend to make breads taste too sweet. Also, take note that the amount of calcium and vitamin D varies in these products. If milk substitutes make an important contribution to your daily requirement of these nutrients, read the labels carefully.

Good Flat Bread

This bread is quick, easy to prepare and ideal in a brown-bag lunch. Reheating in a microwave, at home or in the office, greatly improves the flavor. I like to add a variety of seasonings to this bread, such as olives and pepperoni. It is also popular with my gluten-eating husband.

1¼ cups GF Flour
1¼ cups warm water
2 t sugar
1 T yeast
¼ cup finely ground corn meal, plus 1 T for the pan
1 t salt
1½ t xanthan gum
1 T oil
2 medium eggs or 1 egg and 1 white
1 T ground pepper

Optional added ingredients:
¼ cup chopped green or black olives, drained
¼ cup chopped GF pepperoni, ham or leftover cooked bacon crumbles
1 T minced onion
1 T minced jalapeno pepper

1. Preheat oven to 400°.
2. Place ½ cup of GF flour into a small bowl with the yeast, sugar and a ½ cup hot water. Mix and let rise about 5 minutes.
3. Put remaining GF flour, the ¼ cup of corn meal, salt and xanthan gum in a big bowl. Add eggs, oil and remaining hot water; lightly mix.
4. Add yeast mixture and beat for 4 minutes.
5. Add the olives, meat and other seasonings and blend slowly until the mixture is well mixed.
6. Oil a 9 x 13 inch baking pan with cooking spray and lightly sprinkle the remaining 1 tablespoon corn meal over the pan. Pour the batter into the prepared pan and spread evenly. Let the mixture rise 5 minutes before baking. Bake for about 20 to 25 minutes, until crispy and browned. Enjoy the bread warm or freeze in serving-size squares for packed lunches.

NUTRITIONAL STATS Servings 12, Serving size 34 g, Calories 110, Calories from fat 20, Fat 2.5 g, Saturated fat 0 g, Cholesterol 20 mg, Sodium 110 mg, Carbohydrate 19 g, Fiber 3 g, Protein 3 g

Polenta

When I was a girl, my grandfather came to live with my family when he was in his 90s. I remember that one of his favorite foods was corn-meal mush cooled until firm in a loaf pan, then sliced and fried in butter. He enjoyed this concoction with maple syrup for breakfast. It seemed pretty weird to me at the time, so it is amazing to realize that today, something similar (minus the syrup and butter) is served with a fine tomato sauce as a main course in excellent restaurants.

When my husband, our three children and their spouses, fiancés and friends took a vacation to Scotland, each family group took responsiblity for one evening meal. Josh and his two college friends made an excellent polenta with roasted vegetables and lots of olive oil that I include here. Not exactly corn-meal mush with maple syrup, but pretty good all the same.

Stirred Polenta

1 cup corn meal, may be called corn grits, medium or coarse grind
4 cups water
1 t salt

1. Bring the water to a boil in a large saucepan.
2. Slowly stir in the corn meal and salt. Once the corn meal combines with the water, reduce the heat to simmer.
3. Continue stirring while the mixture simmers, uncovered, for 20 to 25 minutes or until stiff. The mixture gets even firmer as it cools. Serve immediately or place in an oiled pan and chill until it is firm enough to slice.

NUTRITIONAL STATS Servings 4, Serving size 239 g, Calories 160, Calories from fat 0, Fat 0 g, Saturated fat 0 g, Cholesterol 0 mg, Sodium 580 mg, Carbohydrate 36 g, Fiber 4 g, Protein 4 g

Yes-You-Can Baked Polenta

When my friend Kate told me you could save yourself all that stirring and make baked polenta, I did not believe her. But she was right. Try it yourself and see.

Preheat the oven to 375º. Lightly oil a 9 x 9 baking dish. Following ingredient list from Stirred Polenta, pour the water and salt in the pan and sprinkle the corn meal over the top. Stir to combine and place in the oven. Bake for about 45 minutes. Stir once or twice during baking.

Josh's Polenta with Roasted Vegetables

2 cloves garlic
1 medium red onion, sliced in slivers
3 carrots, peeled and sliced in small pieces
1 small eggplant, peeled and cubed
1 summer squash, peeled and cubed
10 leaves of basil, chopped
½ cup olive oil
Prepared Stirred Polenta

1. Preheat the oven to 425º.
2. Pour about ¼ cup olive oil over the bottom of a 9 x 13 inch roasting pan.
3. Spread the vegetables evenly over the pan, salt and pepper and drizzle the remaining oil over the top. Stir to mix.
4. Bake for about 45 minutes in the upper third of the oven so that the vegetables brown. While the veggies are roasting, prepare polenta.
5. Remove the vegetables from the pan and scrape the bottom of the pan to remove any charred bits.
6. Lightly mash the vegetables leaving some chunks.
7. Stir the roasted vegetables into the prepared polenta.
8. Serve immediately or cool and serve later.

Serving note: This dish is good reheated or served at room temperature. Or make it a day ahead, slice and reheat in the oven. Lightly brush with olive oil before reheating for about 10 to 15 minutes in a 375º oven.

NUTRITIONAL STATS Servings 10, Serving size 129 g, Calories 180, Calories from fat 110, Fat 12 g, Saturated fat 1.5 g, Cholesterol 0 g, Sodium 20 mg, Carbohydrate 17 g, Fiber 3 g, Protein 2 g

Heather's Favorite German-Style Oven Pancake

MOLLY RECALLS: Heather always used to ask for oven pancake for her birthday or special-occasion breakfasts. While I enjoyed eating oven pancake, too, my favorite part was watching the pancake puff up like a balloon in the oven. I have to admit, I always felt a little disappointed when it settled on my plate. But the powdered sugar helped.

3 eggs
¼ cup GF flour
2 T GF/DF margarine
½ cup rice, soy or almond milk
1 t GF almond or vanilla flavoring
3 T powdered sugar
1 lemon cut in wedges

Optional: 2 cups fresh fruit, such as strawberries or raspberries

1. Preheat oven to 450° or 425° if using a glass pan.
2. In a mixing bowl, combine the eggs and milk with fork.
3. Slowly blend in the flour.
4. Melt the margarine and add it to the egg, milk and flour mixture.
5. Stir in the flavoring. The batter will be slightly lumpy. Do not over beat.
6. Grease ovenproof pie pan.
7. Pour the batter into the pan.
8. Bake for 15 minutes; drop heat to 350° and bake for 7 minutes more. Do not open oven door while the pancake is baking. The pancake puffs up while cooking and gets nicely browned on top. It begins to fall the minute you remove it from the oven.
8. Serve pancake immediately with powdered sugar and lemon wedges, or fresh fruit.

NUTRITIONAL STATS Servings 3, Serving size 43 g, Calories 250, Calories from fat 120, Fat 13 g, Saturated fat 4 g, Cholesterol 210 mg, Sodium 160 mg, Carbohydrate 25 g, Fiber 1 g, Protein 8 g

Carrot Muffins

2 cups GF flour
½ t salt
4 t baking powder
1½ t xanthan gum
Zest of one orange
¾ cup sugar
2 eggs
⅓ cup canola oil
¾ cup milk substitute
1 cup shredded carrots
⅓ cup dried cranberries
½ cup chopped walnuts

1. Preheat the oven to 400°. Prepare a pan to bake 12 muffins by lining it with paper muffin liners.
2. In a medium-size bowl, combine the flour, salt, baking powder, xanthan gum, orange zest and sugar. Stir dry ingredients to blend.
3. Add eggs, milk substitute and oil, and beat until ingredients are blended. Stir in the carrots, cranberries and walnuts.
4. Fill prepared muffin pans about half full. Place in the bottom one third of the oven. Bake for 20 minutes or until the muffins are firm and lightly browned.
5. Place the muffin pans on cooling racks and remove the muffins from the pans.

NUTRITIONAL STATS Servings 12, Serving size 87 g, Calories 250, Calories from fat 90, Fat 11 g, Saturated fat 1 g, Cholesterol 0 g, Sodium 270 mg, Carbohydrate 38 g, Fiber 3 g, Protein 4 g

Gus' Blueberry Muffins

When our first grandson was one year old, he came to spend a week while his parents had to travel for work. It was a fun-filled visit, but we always worried that Gus did not eat much—except for his very favorite food, blueberries. So blueberry muffins became a big hit and a sure way to get the little guy to eat breakfast.

½ cup GF/DF margarine
¾ cup sugar
2 eggs
1 t baking powder
1 t baking soda
1½ t xanthan gum
½ T lemon zest
Juice of 1 large lemon and almond milk to make ½ cup liquid
2 cup GF flour
1 t almond flavoring
1 pint fresh blueberries, washed, remove stems or any unripe berries

1. Preheat oven to 375°. Place paper muffin liners in 12 muffin cups.
2. In a medium bowl, beat the margarine and sugar until well blended. Add the eggs and continue beating until mixture is light and fluffy.
3. In a separate bowl, combine the baking powder, baking soda, xanthan gum, zest and flour. Stir until well combined. Add the dry ingredients to the egg mixture. Pour the lemon juice and almond milk over the dry ingredients and beat until the entire mixture is blended completely.
4. Stir in the blueberries and fill muffin tins ½ to ¾ full.
5. Bake for 30 minutes or until the muffins are lightly browned and firm to touch.
6. Remove from the oven and cool for a few minutes in muffin pans. Then remove from pans and cool completely on racks.

NUTRITIONAL STATS Servings 12, Serving size 89 g, Calories 220, Calories from fat 80, Fat 9 g, Saturated fat 2.5 g, Cholesterol 35 mg, Sodium 220 mg, Carbohydrate 34 g, Fiber 2 g, Protein 4 g

Desserts

The offerings in our desserts chapter are gluten-free and dairy-free but not sugar-free. A number of the recipes use chopped and ground nuts in place of flour, and egg whites frequently make the ingredients list. While some of these recipes do not use any flour, having gluten-free flour on hand makes baking easier. Add one of the good commercially available GF baking flours to your pantry or prepare the GF flour blend from our *Breads* chapter.

Using nuts and nut meal

Roasted nuts are featured often in these dessert recipes. We recommend buying plain fresh raw nuts and oven-roasting them yourself. The process is easy. Spread a single layer of nuts on a jelly roll pan and bake for 10 minutes at 350°. Cool and place in a freezer bag and freeze until ready to use.

If you buy commercially roasted nuts, read the labels carefully. Many contain a lot of salt. New labeling laws help identify when the risk of cross-contamination is present, something many intolerants learned by unfortunate experience before the new labels were in effect.

You can substitute nut meal, composed of finely ground nuts, for some of the flour in most of these dessert recipes. We generally use from two tablespoons to a quarter-cup of nut meal for part of the regular GF flour. Nut meal provides fiber and enhances the flavor of many desserts. Nut flours or nut meal are expensive and add extra fat to a recipe so it is best to use them in moderation.

Preparing baking pans

When we indicate using a "prepared" baking pan in a recipe, that means we spray or grease the pan, or use one that is nonstick. We like to use commercial sprays to prepare regular baking pans. Read labels carefully as some sprays contain wheat. Another option is lightly spreading a small amount of shortening or margarine over the bottom of the pan. New bakeware designed for nonstick baking does not need oiling. Read your pan instructions and select a method that works for your family.

MOLLY REMEMBERS: We are a family of dessert lovers. Growing up, our cookie jar was filled with random junk—old shoelaces, pencils and napkin rings—because the sweets never seemed to stay on the plate for enough time to make it to the jar. While there have been some disasters in GF treats, with persistence and patience (especially from my father, who was the guinea pig for many test runs), Mom has come up with some really tasty sweets.

Hazelnut Bars

2 cups hazelnuts
1½ cups GF flour
½ cup GF/DF margarine or solid vegetable shortening
½ cup brown sugar
1 egg
1 t xanthan gum
1 12-oz bag GF/DF chocolate chips
½ cup white corn syrup
2 T vanilla almond milk

1. Preheat the oven to 350°.
2. Place the hazelnuts on a cookie sheet and roast for 10 minutes.
3. Remove the nuts from the oven and place them on a clean dish towel. Rub nuts together so that most of the husks are loosened.
4. Put cooled nuts in a bowl and discard the husks. A few husks left on nuts are OK.
5. Mix flour, margarine, brown sugar, egg and xanthan gum together with a mixer until well blended.
6. Press the mixture in prepared 9 x 13 inch baking pan and bake for 18 minutes. Remove from the oven and let the crust cool.
7. In a medium-size saucepan over low heat, melt the corn syrup, milk substitute and chocolate chips.
8. When the crust is cool, spread the melted chocolate mixture on the crust and top with the roasted hazelnuts.
9. When the bars are cool, cut in squares. Store in the refrigerator in an airtight container.

NUTRITIONAL STATS Servings 24, Serving size 66 g, Calories 310, Calories from fat 180, Fat 20 g, Saturated fat 4 g, Cholesterol 10 mg, Sodium 55 mg, Carbohydrate 33 g, Fiber 3 g, Protein 5 g

The long and short on shortening

These dessert recipes call for gluten- and dairy-free margarine or solid vegetable shortening. Dairy-free margarine is not always easy to find. Look in the grocery dairy case near the soy milk or soy cheese products or where other specialty or organic dairy-substitute foods are shelved. Some brands of unsalted margarine may be dairy-free but, again, read the label carefully.

Easy One-Bowl Brownies

1 cup canola oil
2 cups sugar
3 large eggs
1 cup GF flour
½ cup GF cocoa
1 t xanthan gum
1 cup chopped walnuts or pecans

1. Preheat the oven to 350°. Prepare a 9 x 13 inch baking pan.
2. In a medium-size mixing bowl, beat together the canola oil and sugar.
3. Add the eggs and beat well.
4. Mix in the flour, cocoa and xanthan gum, and beat until well mixed.
5. Stir in the nuts. Place the mixture in the pan and bake for 25 minutes.
6. Cool and cut into squares.

NUTRITIONAL STATS Servings 24, Serving size 36 g, Calories 170, Calories from fat 110, Fat 12 g, Saturated fat 1 g, Cholesterol 20 mg, Sodium 10 mg, Carbohydrate 17 g, Fiber 1 g, Protein 2 g

Blonde Brownies

1 cup canola oil
2 cups brown sugar
3 large eggs
1 t xanthan gum
1 t GF baking powder
2 cups GF flour
1 t vanilla
1 cup chopped nuts
1 cup GF/DF chocolate chips

1. Preheat the oven to 350°. Prepare a 9 x 13 inch baking pan.
2. Put the canola oil and brown sugar in a bowl and beat to combine.
3. Add the eggs and beat well.
4. Mix in the flour, xanthan gum, baking powder and vanilla, and beat until well mixed.
5. Stir in the nuts and chocolate chips. Place the mixture in the pan and bake for 25 minutes. Let bars cool completely before removing them from the pan.

NUTRITIONAL STATS Servings 24, Serving size 52 g, Calories 230, Calories from fat 110, Fat 12 g, Saturated fat 3.5 g, Cholesterol 20 mg, Sodium 95 mg, Carbohydrate 30 g, Fiber 1 g, Protein 3 g

Lane's Bakery Nutty Crunchy Bars

Lane's Bakery is a popular, long-established bakery in Madison, Wisconsin. I picked this recipe up a few years ago when Lane's shared it in a local newspaper. It was easy to convert it to a gluten- and dairy-free recipe by using GF crispy rice cereal. I often serve these to gluten-tolerant eaters and get raves.

1 cup peanuts or other favorite nut
½ cup sugar
1 cup white corn syrup
1 T water
1 t GF vanilla
2 cups peanut butter
4 cups GF crispy rice cereal

1. Preheat oven to 350°. Prepare a 9 x 13 inch baking pan.
2. Spread the peanuts over the bottom of a cookie sheet and place in the oven. Stir frequently until the nuts are golden brown, about 10 minutes. Remove at once and transfer to a cool surface.
3. Heat sugar, corn syrup and water to 100 degrees, or until sugar dissolves and the ingredients mix together.
4. Add the vanilla, peanut butter and nuts; mix lightly.
5. Add the cereal and mix lightly until the cereal is coated completely with the peanut mixture. Pour into the pan and refrigerate until cold. Frost with chocolate frosting if desired.

NUTRITIONAL STATS Servings 24, Serving size 57 g, Calories 240, Calories from fat 110, Fat 12 g, Saturated fat 3.5 g, Cholesterol 20 mg, Sodium 95 mg, Carbohydrate 33 g, Fiber 1 g, Protein 3 g

Note: Nutritional stats do not include frosting.

Optional Crunchy Bars Frosting

2 T margarine
2 cups powdered sugar
¼ cup cocoa
2 - 4 T milk substitute

1. Put the margarine, powdered sugar, cocoa, and 2 tablespoons milk in a small mixing bowl.
2. Mix with mixer until smooth and creamy. Add additional milk a tablespoon at a time if the mixture is too thick.
3. Spread on cooled bars.

Basic Chocolate Chip Cookies

1 cup GF/DF margarine or shortening
1 cup brown sugar
½ cup white sugar
2 medium eggs
1 t xanthan gum
1 t GF baking soda
1 t vanilla
2½ cups GF flour
2 T GF cornstarch
½ cup chopped nuts
1 cup GF/DF chocolate chips

1. Preheat oven to 375º. Position the oven rack in the top one third of the oven.
2. Blend margarine and sugars together.
3. Add eggs and vanilla to sugar mixture.
4. Mix together flour, cornstarch, baking soda and xanthan gum, and add to sugar mixture. Mix well.
5. Add the nuts and chocolate chips and stir to combine until the batter is stiff. *Test dough by baking one cookie. If it does not hold its shape, add flour a tablespoon at a time.*
6. Drop by teaspoons onto a prepared cookie sheet. Bake for 10 minutes. Cool for 2 or 3 minutes on the cookie sheet before removing to cooling racks.

NUTRITIONAL STATS Servings 54, Serving size 24 g, Calories 110, Calories from fat 50, Fat 6 g, Saturated fat 2 g, Cholesterol 5 mg, Sodium 70 mg, Carbohydrate 14 g, Fiber 1 g, Protein 1 g

Easy Sesame Almond Cookies

1½ cups sesame seeds
¾ cup sliced almonds
2 egg whites
½ cup sugar

1. Preheat the oven to 350º.
2. Combine the egg whites and sugar and lightly whisk with a fork until well combined. Do not beat.
3. Add in the sesame seeds and almonds. Stir until combined and the batter is thick.
4. Drop by teaspoons onto a prepared large cookie sheet. Lightly flatten the cookies with a fork and bake for 15 minutes.

NUTRITIONAL STATS Servings 36, Serving size 11 g, Calories 50, Calories from fat 35, Fat 4 g, Saturated fat 0 g, Cholesterol 0 g, Sodium 15 mg, Carbohydrate 3 g, Fiber 1 g, Protein 2 g

Peanut Butter Cookies

¾ cup GF/DF margarine
¾ cup peanut butter
1½ cups brown sugar
¼ cup white sugar
2 medium eggs
1 t xanthan gum
1 t vanilla
2½ cups GF flour
1 t baking powder
½ cup peanuts or other nuts, chopped

1. Preheat oven to 375°.
2. In a large bowl, cream the margarine, peanut butter and brown sugar together.
3. Add eggs, xanthan gum and vanilla, and mix well.
4. Stir in flour, baking powder and nuts until batter is thick.
5. Place white sugar in a small bowl.
6. Form the dough into walnut-size balls, dip in the white sugar and place on a prepared cookie tray. *Test one cookie before baking the entire batch. If it does not hold its shape, add more flour, 1 to 2 tablespoons at a time.*
7. Using a fork, gently flatten the cookies by making a crisscross pattern on the cookie. Bake in the top one-third of the oven for 8 to 10 minutes on a prepared cookie sheet. Let the cookies sit for 3 or 4 minutes before removing them carefully to cooling racks.

NUTRITIONAL STATS Servings 48, Serving size 26 g, Calories 120, Calories from fat 50, Fat 6 g, Saturated fat 1.5 g, Cholesterol 10 mg, Sodium 60 mg, Carbohydrate 14 g, Fiber 1 g, Protein 2 g

Rolled and Frosted Cookies

The next three "intolerant" dessert treats are variations on the same basic cookie recipe. Heather first started baking Mexican Wedding Cakes when she was a young girl. She always placed the cookie in holly-decorated, mini-muffin paper liner for an attractive addition to the holiday cookie tray. The poppy seed version is adapted from a long-time family favorite.

Mexican Wedding Cakes

¾ cup GF/DF margarine
1½ cups powdered sugar
1 cup GF flour
½ cup tapioca flour
1 t xanthan gum
1 medium egg
½ cup chopped nuts
Additional large pieces of nuts for topping cookies

1. Preheat oven to 300°.
2. Combine shortening and sugar in a mixer bowl and mix until well blended.
3. Turn off the mixer and add the flours and xanthan gum. Slowly mix until combined.
4. Add the egg and mix on medium speed for 2 minutes, until the batter is very thick.
5. Add the nuts and stir with a spoon until distributed evenly through the batter.
6. Using your hands, roll about a teaspoon of dough into a small ball and test bake one cookie. The cookie should spread slightly but if it does not hold its shape, add additional GF flour, 1 to 2 tablespoons at a time.
7. Finish making the dough balls and place them on the cookie sheet, spaced about 1½ inches apart.

8. Bake in the lower third of oven for 25 to 30 minutes, or until cookies are firm. Cool on baking sheet for about 2 minutes. Remove from the cookie sheet and cool completely on a rack.
9. Frost with Mexican Wedding Cake Frosting and top each cookie with one nut.

Mexican Wedding Cake Frosting

3 T GF/DF margarine or butter
2 cups powdered sugar
2 - 4 T milk substitute
1 t almond extract

1. Melt the margarine over low heat until bubbly.
2. Place powdered sugar in a small bowl and add the melted margarine, almond extract and 2 tablespoons milk substitute.
3. Mix with an electric mixer until well blended. If necessary, add additional milk until the frosting is of spreading consistency.
4. Frost each cookie and place one nut on top of the frosting. The frosting hardens as it cools so work quickly.

NUTRITIONAL STATS Servings 48, Serving size 25 g, Calories 110, Calories from fat 40, Fat 4.5 g, Saturated fat 1 g, Cholesterol 5 mg, Sodium 40 mg, Carbohydrate 17 g, Fiber 0, Protein 1 g

Note: Nutritional stats include frosting.

Poppy Seed Cookies

¾ cup GF/DF margarine
1½ cups powdered sugar
1 cup GF flour
½ cup tapioca flour
1 t xanthan gum
1 medium egg
½ cup poppy seeds

1. Preheat the oven to 300°.
2. Combine shortening and sugar in a mixer bowl and mix until well blended.
3. Turn off the mixer and add the flours and xanthan gum. Slowly mix until combined.
4. Add the egg and mix on medium speed for 2 minutes, until the batter is very thick.
5. Add the poppy seeds and stir until evenly distributed throughout the batter.
6. Using your hands, roll about a teaspoon of dough into a small ball and test bake one cookie. The cookie should spread slightly but if it does not hold its shape, add additional GF flour, 1 to 2 tablespoons at a time.
7. Finish making the dough balls and place them on the cookie sheet, spaced about 1½ inches apart.
8. Bake in the lower third of oven for 25 to 30 minutes, or until cookies are firm. Cool on baking sheet for about 2 minutes. Remove and cool completely on a rack.
9. When the cookies are cool, frost with Chocolate Frosting.

Chocolate Frosting

2 T GF/DF margarine
1 cup powdered sugar
2 T GF cocoa powder
1 - 2 T GF/DF milk substitute

1. In a small mixing bowl, combine the shortening with the powdered sugar and cocoa.
1. Beat until well combined.
1. Add 1 tablespoon of milk or more if needed so the frosting is of spreading consistency. Put a small dab of frosting on each cookie.

NUTRITIONAL STATS Servings 48, Serving size 20 g, Calories 90, Calories from fat 40, Fat 4 g, Saturated fat 1 g, Cholesterol 5 mg, Sodium 35 mg, Carbohydrate 12 g, Fiber 0, Protein 1 g

Note: Nutritional stats include frosting.

Chocolate Pecan Cookies

¾ cup GF/DF margarine
1½ cups brown sugar
1 cup GF flour
½ cup tapioca flour
½ cup cocoa powder
1 t xanthan gum
1 medium egg
¾ cup chopped pecans

1. Preheat oven to 300°.
2. Combine shortening and sugar in a mixer bowl and mix until well blended.
3. Turn off mixer and add the flours, cocoa and xanthan gum. Slowly mix until combined.
4. Add the egg and mix on medium speed for 2 minutes, until the batter is very thick.
5. Add nuts and stir until distributed evenly through batter.
6. Using your hands, roll about a teaspoon of dough into a small ball and test bake one cookie. The cookie should spread slightly but if it does not hold its shape, add additional GF flour, 1 to 2 tablespoons at a time.
7. Finish making the dough balls and place them on the cookie sheet, spaced about 1½ inches apart.
8. Bake in the lower third of the oven for 25 to 30 minutes. Cool cookies on the baking sheet for about 2 minutes. Remove and cool completely on a rack.
9. Roll in powdered sugar or frost with Chocolate Frosting, pg. 120.

NUTRITIONAL STATS Servings 48, Serving size 18 g, Calories 80, Calories from fat 40, Fat 4.5 g, Saturated fat 1 g, Cholesterol 5 mg, Sodium 30 mg, Carbohydrate 11 g, Fiber 1 g, Protein 1 g

Best Chocolate Pudding

Like many Midwesterners, I belonged to 4-H as a youngster. One activity I remember fondly was the foods project, maybe because I saved my "It's Fun to Cook" cookbook from that time. Inside is a simple recipe for a steamed chocolate pudding that our family enjoyed for years. The recipe works almost as well with milk substitutes and, since it has no eggs, it is a good choice for those intolerant to eggs. I have used rice milk, almond milk and coconut milk to prepare the pudding and find that the almond or coconut works best. The coconut milk is the least-healthy option.

2¾ cup vanilla almond milk, rice milk or other milk substitute
½ cup sugar
3 T cocoa
6 T cornstarch
1 T GF/DF margarine
1 t GF almond or vanilla flavoring

1. In a double boiler saucepan, heat 2 cups of the DF milk.
2. In a small bowl, combine the remaining milk with the sugar, cocoa and cornstarch; stir until the mixture is smooth.
3. When the milk on the stove is warm, slowly stir in the cocoa mixture and continue stirring until the pudding thickens, about 5 to 7 minutes.
4. When the pudding begins to thicken, cover and continue to cook for 15 minutes. Do not stir and do not remove the cover.
5. After 15 minutes, remove the saucepan from the heat and stir in the margarine and almond or vanilla flavoring.
6. Place in individual serving dishes. Serve warm or refrigerate and serve later.

NUTRITIONAL STATS Servings 5, Serving size 163 g, Calories 150, Calories from fat 35, Fat 4 g, Saturated fat 1 g, Cholesterol 0 mg, Sodium 110 mg, Carbohydrate 29 g, Fiber 1 g, Protein 1 g

Coconut Banana Custard

MOLLY RECALLS: I like bananas and their sweetness reduces the need for sugar in desserts and baked products. This pudding is like the tapioca pudding Mom made when we were kids. Adding the bananas gives you the nutritional advantages of the fruit while using less sugar.

1 cup canned unsweetened coconut milk
1 cup water
¼ cup tapioca pearls
½ cup sugar
Pinch of salt
1½ ripe bananas, peeled and diced
1½ T toasted sesame seeds for garnish

1. In a saucepan, bring the coconut milk and water to boil.
2. Reduce the heat to medium low and stir in the tapioca, sugar and salt.
3. Cook until the tapioca pearls are translucent, about 30 minutes.
4. Add the bananas and cook for 10 minutes more.
5. Spoon into serving dishes and garnish with sesame seeds.

NUTRITIONAL STATS Servings 4, Serving size 190 g, Calories 260, Calories from fat 120, Fat 14 g, Saturated fat 11 g, Cholesterol 0 mg, Sodium 15 mg, Carbohydrate 39 g, Fiber 2 g, Protein 2 g

Frozen Desserts

It has been years since I have eaten ice cream and I do miss it sometimes. My yearning might have to do with growing up in the Dairy State or living next to a university campus where they make some of the best ice cream in the world. I always counted on ice cream sundaes as a quick dessert I knew all our guests would love. Well, my guests still can enjoy their sundaes, even if my food intolerance means I cannot. But now, when I do crave a frozen dessert, I am pleased to have more choices.

GF/DF frozen desserts are available in the frozen foods section of specialty stores and large supermarkets. These include sorbets, and soy- and rice-based frozen products. Read labels carefully to ensure the absence of both dairy and gluten. The sorbet recipe is quick and easy to prepare at the end of a busy day. The recipe for lemon ice uses gelatin and requires beating with a mixer twice during preparation. The easiest way to do this is to freeze the dessert in a round plastic freezer container so you can use a hand-held mixer right in the freezer container.

Quick and Easy Strawberry or Raspberry Sorbet

1 lb bag of unsweetened frozen strawberries or raspberries, slightly thawed
½ cup white wine
1 cup orange juice
½ cup sugar

1. Place all the ingredients in a food processor and blend until pureed.
2. Serve immediately or place the puree in a freezer container and freeze until partially firm, about 1 hour.
3. Remove from freezer and mix with an electric mixer until mixture is smooth but still frozen.
4. If not using immediately, replace mixture in the freezer container and freeze until firm, about another hour.
5. Remove from the freezer about 10 minutes before serving and allow the sorbet to soften slightly before serving. Suitable for freezing overnight but it is best when eaten in two days.

NUTRITIONAL STATS Servings 6, Serving size 153 g, Calories 120, Calories from fat 5, Fat 0 g, Saturated fat 0 g, Cholesterol 0 mg, Sodium 0 mg, Carbohydrate 27 g, Fiber 2 g, Protein 1 g

Lemon Ice

Lemon ice was a summer treat our family enjoyed before the dairy-free days. It is refreshing on a hot day. In a rush, you can use bottled lemon juice instead of squeezing fresh lemons. But we find the flavor is better with the fresh-squeezed.

6 large lemons, use juice of all 6 and zest of 2 lemons
1 envelope unflavored gelatin
1 cup sugar
2½ cups water

1. Juice the lemons to about ¾ cup of lemon juice.
2. Zest two of the lemons and retain the zest.
3. Put the water, gelatin and sugar in a saucepan and heat over medium heat, stirring constantly until the gelatin and sugar dissolve.
4. Remove the saucepan from the heat and stir in the lemon juice and zest.
5. Pour the mixture in a freezer container and freeze about an hour or until the mixture is firm.
6. Remove from the freezer and beat with a mixer until thick and fluffy.
7. Replace in the freezer dish and refreeze for another 2 hours. Remove from the freezer and beat again with electric mixer.
8. When mixture is smooth, return the sorbet to the freezer and freeze until firm, another 2 hours. When ready to serve, remove the sorbet from the freezer 10 or 15 minutes before serving to let it soften.

NUTRITIONAL STATS Servings 6, Serving size 153 g, Calories 90, Calories from fat 0, Fat 0 g, Saturated Fat 0 g, Cholesterol 0 mg, Sodium 0 mg, Carbohydrate 27 g, Fiber 0 g, Protein 0 g

Chocolate Nut Cake with Creamy Chocolate Frosting

This cake is unbelievably good and your guests will never guess it is gluten-free. But the real find here is the frosting. When my children were young, red cakes were popular—cakes made with lots of red food coloring, a small amount of cocoa and topped with a cooked frosting that contained lots of well-beaten Crisco. This frosting adapts well to GF, DF baking, although I sometimes call it "eating Crisco" and cannot vouch for its nutritional value. But once in a while, having a frosting that looks and tastes rich and creamy makes up for all those wedding, birthday and special-event cakes you must decline.

¾ cup GF/DF margarine
2 cups white sugar
4 eggs
½ cup cocoa, or ¾ cup for a stronger chocolate flavor
2½ cups finely chopped nuts
½ cup GF flour
1½ t xanthan gum
1 cup GF/DF milk substitute

1. Preheat the oven to 350°, prepare two 9-inch round pans.
2. Cream margarine with the sugar until light and fluffy.
3. Add the eggs and continue beating until the mixture is light and fluffy.
4. Blend the cocoa and GF flour together and add to the beaten mixture alternately with the milk, blending during each addition.
5. Fold in the nuts.
6. Divide the batter between the two pans and bake for about 30 minutes, until cake is done. Remove from the oven and cool on racks.
7. Frost layers, top and sides with Creamy Chocolate Frosting.

Creamy Chocolate Frosting or Eating Crisco

1 cup GF milk substitute
1½ T cornstarch
1 8-oz bar GF/DF bittersweet chocolate
1½ cup Crisco
1½ cup sugar

1. Place ¾ cup of milk substitute in a small saucepan and warm.
2. Mix the cornstarch with the remaining milk substitute

and slowly add to the milk in the pan, stirring constantly.
3. Break up the chocolate and add to the milk mixture.
4. Stir until the chocolate is melted and milk mixture becomes thick. Set aside to cool.
5. In a mixing bowl, combine the sugar and the Crisco. Beat at high speed for 5 minutes, until the mixture is light and fluffy. Beat in the cooled chocolate mixture and blend to mix completely. This makes enough frosting to fill one layer, and frost the sides and top of the cake.

NUTRITIONAL STATS Servings 16, Serving size 143 g, Calories 590, Calories from fat 360, Fat 40 g, Saturated fat 9 g, Cholesterol 55 mg, Sodium 120 mg, Carbohydrate 55 g, Fiber 2 g, Protein 6 g

Note: Nutritional stats represent both cake and frosting.

Great Pumpkin Dessert

In all my years of cooking, I never *ever* made a good pie crust. Whenever we needed a pie crust, either Heather made it or I bought one in the frozen foods section and snuck it in the back door (figuratively speaking). So when I became gluten intolerant, I did not even try to produce a GF crust. Instead, I adapted a favorite pumpkin dessert into a delicious gluten- and dairy-free option. I add lots of nuts so no one misses the butter.

1 cup GF flour
1¼ cups sugar
½ cup GF/DF margarine
1½ cups chopped walnuts or pecans
1 15-oz can solid-pack pumpkin
1½ cups GF/DF milk substitute
3 eggs

1. Preheat oven to 350°.
2. In medium bowl, blend the flour, ¾ cup sugar, margarine and nuts together with a fork. Mixture resembles large crumbs.
3. In another mixing bowl, combine pumpkin, milk substitute, eggs and remaining sugar.
4. Pour pumpkin mixture into prepared 9 x 13 baking pan. Sprinkle with crumb mixture. Bake for 1 hour, or until knife inserted near the center comes out clean.

NUTRITIONAL STATS Servings 12, Serving size 137 g, Calories 330, Calories from fat 170, Fat 19 g, Saturated fat 3.5 g, Cholesterol 55 mg, Sodium 120 mg, Carbohydrate 37 g, Fiber 3 g, Protein 6 g

Angel Food Cake with Blueberry Sauce

This cake is easier than you think and makes a great GF/DF dessert. And, despite its simple, inexpensive ingredients, an angel food cake always impresses. Lightly sweetened fresh berries or peaches are an excellent way to accompany an angel food cake. A cooked fruit sauce, like the one featured here, makes a plain slice of cake seem special.

10 egg whites from large eggs
1½ t cream of tartar
½ t salt
2 cups sugar
¾ cup GF flour, sifted with tapioca flour
¼ cup tapioca flour
1 t xanthan gum

1. Preheat oven to 375°.
2. Sift the flours and xanthan gum together in a small bowl. Set aside.
3. Put egg whites in a large mixer bowl and mix at medium speed. When foamy, add the salt and cream of tartar.
4. Add the sugar to the egg whites, 1 heaping tablespoon at a time and continue beating at high speed until all the sugar is mixed in. The whites will be thick and glossy with peaks that fold over softly.
5. Carefully fold the flour mixture into the egg whites, adding about ⅓ of the flour mixture at a time. Do this by sprinkling each portion of the dry mixture over the egg whites then gently fold it in with a spatula. When all the flour is folded in, carefully pour the mixture into an ungreased tube pan and bake for 50 minutes. The cake should be nicely browned with cracks on top and spring back when lightly touched.
6. Remove from oven and cool completely with the tube pan turned upside down. When cool, run a knife around the sides of pan and lightly tap the pan bottom. If necessary, run the knife along the bottom. The cake should ease out of the pan.

NUTRITIONAL STATS Servings 16, Serving size 59 g, Calories 150, Calories from fat 5, Fat 0 g, Saturated fat 0 g, Cholesterol 0 mg, Sodium 110 mg, Carbohydrate 35 g, Fiber 1 g, Protein 3 g

Blueberry or Other Berry Sauce

2 pints of berries
1 cup orange juice
⅓ cup white wine
½ cup sugar
1 T lime juice
1 T cornstarch

1. In a small saucepan, place ¾ cup of orange juice, the sugar and wine and heat until warm.
2. Combine cornstarch with remaining orange juice and stir into warm liquids. Stir until mixture begins to thicken.
3. Take 1 cup of the berries and squash lightly with a fork. Stir the squashed berries into the sauce and continue cooking for about 5 minutes until sauce thickens.
4. Add remaining whole berries and lime juice and cook for 5 minutes more. Serve warm or cold with cake.

NUTRITIONAL STATS Servings 16, Serving size 63 g, Calories 50, Calories from fat 0, Total fat 0 g, Saturated fat 0 g, Cholesterol 0 mg, Sodium 0 mg, Carbohydrate 12 g, Fiber 1 g, Protein 0 g

Peach Crisp

6 large peaches, peeled and sliced
⅓ cup GF/DF margarine
½ cup brown sugar
⅓ cup GF flour
⅓ cup quinoa flakes
½ cup nuts, chopped

1. Preheat the oven to 375º.
2. Prepare an 8 x 8 inch square pan by spraying or lightly greasing.
3. Place the peaches in the pan.
4. Blend the margarine, brown sugar and GF flour together. Add the quinoa flakes and blend until just combined.
5. Stir in the chopped nuts.
6. Sprinkle the topping over the peaches.
7. Bake in the oven for 20 minutes, or until the peaches are soft and juicy and the topping is lightly browned. Serve warm or cold.

NUTRITIONAL STATS Servings 6, Serving size 206 g, Calories 320, Calories from fat 150, Fat 17 g, Saturated fat 4 g, Cholesterol 0 mg, Sodium 110 mg, Carbohydrate 40 g, Fiber 4 g, Protein 4 g

Chocolate Nut Pie

This dessert features another alternative to a rolled pie crust. I use the bar cookie base from the Hazel Nut Bars in this chapter for the crust, pressing it into a pie pan with my fingers rather than rolling it. The filling for this dessert is so rich, it helps that the crust is light and inconspicuous.

Crust
1½ cups GF flour
½ cup GF/DF margarine
½ cup brown sugar
1 egg
1 t xanthan gum

Filling
10 oz of GF/DF bittersweet chocolate bar, broken in pieces or GF/DF semi-sweet chocolate chips
¼ cup GF/DF margarine
2 cups walnuts or pecans, chopped in large pieces
3 large eggs
1 cup light brown sugar, firmly packed
1 cup vanilla almond milk or hazelnut milk

1. Preheat the oven to 350°.
2. Blend the crust ingredients together until mixture is crumbly.
3. Spray a large pie pan or spring-form pan with cooking spray and press the crust mixture on the bottom and sides of the pan. The crust should be thin. Retain any extra crust for another use.
4. Bake the crust for 15 minutes. Remove from the oven and cool. Reduce the heat to 325°.
5. Meanwhile, melt the chocolate and margarine over low heat.
6. Beat the eggs in a medium-size mixing bowl.
7. Add the brown sugar and milk substitute to the eggs.
8. Slowly add the melted mixture and blend to combine. Add the nuts and mix to distribute evenly.
9. Pour the chocolate filling into the prepared crust and return to the oven. Bake at 325° for 1 hour. Remove from the oven and cool on a wire rack.

NUTRITIONAL STATS Servings 12, Serving size 146 g, Calories 570, Calories from fat 310, Fat 34 g, Saturated fat 9 g, Cholesterol 70 mg, Sodium 160 mg, Carbohydrate 65 g, Fiber 4 g, Protein 8 g

Fudge

Growing up in small-town Wisconsin, Marshmallow Fluff was an occasional ingredient in special desserts. The *Never-Fail Fudge* recipe—a fixture on the jar label for as long as I remember—easily adapts to GF/DF baking. We add roasted nuts but they are optional. A candy thermometer, for sale in most grocery stores, is the secret to making good fudge because it is the best way to ensure the mixture reaches the correct temperature.

2½ cups sugar
¼ cup GF/DF margarine
⅔ cup GF/DF milk substitute
1 7.5-oz jar Marshmallow Fluff
1 t GF vanilla
12-oz bag GF/DF semi-sweet chocolate chips
1 cup nuts, optional

1. Combine the sugar, margarine, milk substitute, Marshmallow Fluff and vanilla. Stir over low heat until blended.
2. Increase heat to medium and bring mixture to a boil, stirring constantly. Boil until candy thermometer registers 240° or the soft-ball stage.
3. Remove from the heat and stir in the chocolate and vanilla. Stir until the chocolate is melted.
4. Add nutmeats, if used, and stir to distribute.
5. Pour into a prepared 9 x 9 inch square pan. Refrigerate. When cool, cut into small squares.

NUTRITIONAL STATS Servings 48, Serving size 24 g, Calories 90, Calories from fat 25, Fat 3 g, Saturated fat 1.5 g, Cholesterol 0 mg, Sodium 20 mg, Carbohydrate 16 g, Fiber 1 g, Protein 1 g

Note: Nutritionals stats do not include nuts

Chocolate-Covered Hazelnuts

This is an excellent option for a holiday cookie tray or to serve as a special treat at the end of a special meal when a small bite of something sweet is in order. The nuts are easy to prepare, and they store well for several days in an airtight container or in the freezer. Hazelnuts are a favorite at our house, but whole pecans, walnuts or Brazil nuts make good alternatives. The secret to good flavor is roasting the nuts.

1 lb raw hazelnuts
6 oz of good-quality GF/DF chocolate, bittersweet or semi-sweet chocolate bars

1. Preheat the oven to 350°.
2. Place the hazelnuts on a jelly roll pan in a single layer. Bake in the oven for 10 minutes or until the nuts are lightly browned.
3. Remove from the oven and cool. Then place on a clean tea towel and rub gently until the husks come loose. Some husks may remain on the nuts. Discard the husks.
4. Melt the chocolate in a small saucepan over low heat. When the chocolate is melted, put several nuts at a time into the melted chocolate. Using a teaspoon, lightly stir until the nuts are covered.
5. With a teaspoon, scoop the coated nuts from the pan in clusters of 2 or 3 and place on waxed paper. They will harden into small nut clusters.
6. Repeat until all nuts are dipped. When cool enough, put the clusters in an airtight container and place in the refrigerator to cool further. They are best stored in the refrigerator, or the freezer for longer-term storage.

NUTRITIONAL STATS Servings 40, Serving size 16 g, Calories 90, Calories from fat 70, Fat 8 g, Saturated fat 1 g, Cholesterol 0 mg, Sodium 0 mg, Carbohydrate 5 g, Fiber 1 g, Protein 2 g

Peanut Butter Chocolate Candies or Buckeyes

My sister lived in Ohio for many years where everyone who roots for the Ohio State football team enjoyed a peanut butter-based candy ball called Buckeyes that was dipped in chocolate. My sister's Buckeyes always look perfect with a small circle of peanut butter ball showing through the chocolate coating. My dipping skills are not even close to hers, so I simply coat the peanut butter centers with chocolate. Not quite as attractive as the originals, these eyeless Buckeyes are tasty morsels.

1 cup creamy peanut butter
½ cup finely ground GF cereal
1 cup powdered sugar
2 cups GF/DF semi-sweet chocolate chips
1 T solid vegetable shortening

1. In a food processor, combine the peanut butter, cereal and powdered sugar, and pulse until all ingredients are well blended. Refrigerate until cold, at least an hour.
2. Take teaspoons full of the peanut butter mixture and roll into round balls. Refrigerate until ready to dip in chocolate. Can be prepared ahead and refrigerated overnight.
3. Melt the chocolate and shortening over low heat until the chocolate is liquid. Use a fork or skewer to dip each individual peanut butter ball into chocolate keeping the top of the ball out of the chocolate.
4. Place the candies on waxed paper on a cookie sheet. Refrigerate until firm and store in the refrigerator, or freeze for three to four weeks.

NUTRITIONAL STATS Servings 48, Serving size 19 g, Calories 90, Calories from fat 45, Fat 5 g, Saturated fat 1.5 g, Cholesterol 0 mg, Sodium 20 mg, Carbohydrate 11 g, Fiber 0 g, Protein 0 g

Good Food, Safe Food: Making it Work

At some point after being diagnosed with a food intolerance, most people roll up their sleeves and decide to prepare some or most of their meals at home, even if they had no interest in cooking before.

Planning for myself how to live with and cook in a food-restricted environment, I decided to create a "zone of safety" where the foods eaten are free of things that make you sick. In our home, that means an area where it is easy to prepare foods that are both gluten-free and dairy-free.

While all the food we eat at home is gluten- and dairy-free, we do keep bread, crackers and breakfast cereal on hand for gluten eaters and milk, cheese and butter in the refrigerator. We live in the Dairy State after all!

Such exceptions make the zone of safety an important concept. And since the risk of cross contamination is greatest from ingredients that contain gluten, it is important to establish gluten-free areas for food preparation and food storage.

Our solution is a small counter area for storing bread products that contain gluten and the toaster gluten eaters use to prepare those foods. All work surfaces are gluten-free. We do not keep flours containing gluten in the house. If you must, place them in securely fastened zipper storage bags to avoid accidental consumption. It sounds paranoid, but for some individuals, ingesting even a small amount of airborne wheat particles creates health problems.

Handy appliances

Most gluten intolerants hunger for bread. Even if you never made bread before, it is worth learning how to do it by hand or by machine. A bread machine or a stand mixer makes it easy to incorporate bread baking into a busy schedule. If you plan to bake your own GF breads, purchase either a stand mixer with a 4.5- to 6-quart bowl or a bread machine. Use the stand mixer for cookies, cakes or other desserts, as well as bread.

Both appliances are heavy, a feature that makes them ideal for the job. They also require a good deal of counter and storage space, and are fairly expensive. A lightweight hand mixer is useful for some food preparation, but it will not handle bread batter.

We are big fans of hand blenders. This versatile appliance does a great job of blending soups and sauces. It makes chopping vegetables, and mincing onions and garlic a breeze. But we appreciate it most for preparing fresh and tasty salad dressings in just a few minutes. Hand blenders are dishwasher safe, saving clean-up time.

Good, sharp kitchen knives also are important. They do many of the same things a blender does and some things better. For example, hand blenders may turn tomatoes or other fruits and vegetables to mush when preparing salsas.

Shopping for GF/DF products

There are more sources for specialty foods all the time. If you live in a city, your supermarket probably carries GF flours and milk alternatives. Smaller specialty stores and food co-ops that carry natural or organic foods, and Asian or Mexican markets are good choices, too. If you live near a Trader Joe's or Whole Foods stores, GF choices abound. In-store labeling and the knowledgeable people on staff in these outlets makes shopping easy. For products not available locally, mail and online sources give us access to a wider range of GF and DF foods.

These three websites are a good place to learn more about GF and DF foods sources:
- glutenfreemall.com
- celiac.com
- gluten.net

Purchase a listing of commercially prepared GF foods. It is a helpful tool for shopping and buying healthful, good-tasting alternatives. The Celiac Sprue Association (CSA) publishes and updates these listings regularly. Find them at csaceliacs.org.

Turn reliable brands into favorites

Everyone finds their own favorites as they explore ingredients and food alternatives. Here are a few reliable brands I use regularly.

Pacific Foods brand for milk substitutes and chicken, beef or vegetable stock. Their hazelnut milk is a special treat in your morning coffee. This brand carries dairy substitutes that are not gluten-free but they clearly label the products that are gluten-free and dairy-free. Not all milk substitutes from Pacific Foods are calcium-enriched, so check the labels to find the ones that are.

Almond Breeze almond milk is one of the most widely available GF milk substitutes. The vanilla flavor is great in making puddings or other sweet foods. Almond Breeze is lower in calories and calcium than the Pacific Foods brands. Some stores also carry a sugar-free version.

Penzey's Spices carries superior seasonings. This Wisconsin-based company has an extensive on-line store (penzeys.com) that means you can keep these excellent seasonings on hand wherever you live. When I last checked, the taco seasoning was not gluten-free so read the labels or call the helpful staff for assistance.

Earth Balance is the best GF, DF, no-transfats butter substitute that I have found. So many margarines contain dairy or lack flavor that I almost gave up hope of having "butter" on my freshly baked bread. I use Earth Balance for most of my baking and, unless otherwise specified, it is the margarine product used in the recipes in this book. I find

Earth Balance in the refrigerator section of my regular supermarket near the organic or natural foods. This section also features refrigerated soy milks and cheese substitutes.

Keep pantry well stocked

I grew up in a small town where the grocery store closed early and the one fast food restaurant, an A & W drive-in, was open only in the summer. As a result, my family learned to keep certain foods in the pantry for emergencies. For food intolerants, a well-stocked emergency food shelf is a good idea because you cannot always count on finding GF, DF foods when you crave a substantial snack. Out of frustration, intolerants sometimes eat the wrong foods because quick *healthful* snacks are not available. The days of ordering out for pizza are over!

Emergency food pantry ideas

Here are some ideas of foods to keep on hand for making a last-minute small meal or snack, or serving unexpected guests when there is no time to shop.

- Canned tuna – Stock solid white, canned in either water or olive oil; water pack is lower in fat but the olive oil makes this pantry item a tasty, elegant food for a quick antipasto tray
- Diced tomatoes – Good for soups or emergency salsa
- Mangos – A quick dessert or emergency salsa ingredient
- Artichokes or hearts of palm
- Olives – Both ripe and green
- GF chicken broth
- GF mayo
- Thin rice noodles
- Dried or canned mushrooms
- Roasted red peppers in a jar
- Milk substitute
- Quinoa
- Fish sauce or GF soy sauce
- Wine or cider vinegar
- Peanut butter
- GF/DF corn chips
- Prepared bottled hummus – Read labels carefully, or keep canned garbanzo beans and tahini on shelf to mix from scratch
- GF rice bowls – Easy to prepare in a few minutes
- Roasted nuts – Best stored in the freezer
- Prepared bottled salsa – Read ingredients list carefully
- GF/DF crackers
- Olive oil
- GF/DF tapenades – Good with crackers or as pasta sauce

Intolerant entertaining

Like any other entertaining, "intolerant" entertaining is most fun when the event is simple and uncomplicated. Plan menus with foods you can make ahead to ease last-minute preparation hassles. I never serve separate menus for gluten or dairy eaters, although I may add a cheese tray to a buffet table or offer ice cream in addition to GF/DF sorbet for dessert. And I find it much easier to serve wheat bread to gluten eaters.

The menus that follow offer ideas for hosting your next party based on recipes in this cookbook. All the recipes are easy to prepare and allow time for the hosts to enjoy their guests and good food.

Cocktail Party Prepare the items in this menu ahead, earlier on the day of the party or the night before. Offer your guests selections from two or three choices of GF cocktails or wine, and make sure to have spring water and soda pop on hand as well. I like to have a small sweet at a cocktail party, and fudge or chocolate-covered nuts are a good idea. Rich food is a good match for cocktails as it helps offset the alcohol.
- Hummus
- Spicy Roasted Red Pepper Dip
- Toasted nuts
- Antipasto Tray
- Fresh vegetables and GF crackers for dipping
- Fudge or Chocolate-Covered Hazelnuts
- Ingredients for two or three favorite cocktails and/or wine
- Sparkling water
- Soda

For a more-varied cocktail buffet, add spring rolls or lettuce wraps to the menu.

Chili Party Chili parties are a family favorite with us. We like to offer two kinds of chili and lots of toppings. Make the chili early in the day and greet your guests with the wonderful smell of the chili cooking. Chili parties are informal and interactive, as you serve up the steaming bowls of chili and let guests choose their own toppings. I like to have three courses and serve them buffet style. Have nibbles out for eating with a drink before dinner then put the toppings on the buffet. Following the chili course, place the dessert on the buffet or serving counter. Because the chili is highly seasoned and substantial, make the dessert course light and soothing.

First Course
Gregg's Salsa
Tomatillo Guacamole
Corn chips
Raw veggies

Chili Course
Tomatillo Chili
Chunky Red Chili, either beef or bean

Toppings
Chopped tomatoes
Chopped peppers
Shredded cheese or soy cheese
Chopped lettuce
Guacamole
GF/DF corn chips

Dessert Course
Lemon Ice or commercial GF/DF sorbet
Fruit tray

Sit-Down Dinner Sometimes it is fun to host a more formal, sit-down dinner. This menu is designed to serve in elegant courses, but it is easy to prepare and even easier at serving time. Make the soup early the day of the dinner and reheat after the guests arrive. Assemble and refrigerate the salad ahead. Also prepare, but do not cook, the pork tenderloin early in the day and store in the refrigerator. Place the main-course meat in the oven 45 minutes before the time you plan to serve it. Top the chocolate pie with whipped cream or vanilla ice cream for the dairy-tolerant and offer a scoop of vanilla rice or soy dessert to the dairy-intolerant.

Pear and Leek Soup
Asparagus with Tarragon Vinaigrette
Maple Chili Roasted Pork with carrots
Chocolate Nut Pie

Index

Antipasto
Antipasto, 22

Asparagus
Antipasto, 22
Asparagus with Tarragon Vinaigrette, 55
Roasted Asparagus, 92

Beef
Basic Vegetable Beef Soup, 38
Beef Wrapped in Lettuce, 69
Chunky Red Chili, 32
Curried Beef, 68
Green Tomatillo Chili, 34
Hungarian Goulash, 71
Not Your Mother's Pot Roasted Chicken or Beef, 62
Taco Salad, 44

Blueberry
Angel Food Cake with Blueberry Sauce, 128
Gus' Blueberry Muffins, 109

Bread
Basic Bread, 101
Brown Bread, 102
Corn Bread, 103
Good Flat Bread, ,104

Broccoli
Chicken and Broccoli, 76

Brownie
Blonde Brownies, 114
Easy One-Bowl Brownies, 114

Cabbage
Peanut Cole Slaw, 57
Red Cabbage, 92

Cake
Angel Food Cake with Blueberry Sauce, 128
Chocolate Nut Cake with Creamy Chocolate Frosting, 126

Candy
Chocolate Covered Hazelnuts, 132
Fudge, 131
Peanut Butter Chocolate Candies, 133

Carrot
Carrot and Pineapple Salad, 53
Carrot Curry Soup, 29
Carrot Muffins, 108
Carrot Salad with Lime and Cilantro, 53
Carrot Walnut Salad, 52
Orange Carrot Salad, 52

Cauliflower
Mashed Cauliflower, 90

Chicken
Chicken and Broccoli, 76
Chicken Enchiladas with Salsa Verde, 64
Chicken Pasta Dinner, 65
Chicken Satay with Peanut Sauce, 66
Curried Chicken or Turkey Salad, 48
Lemon Chicken with Ripe and Green Olives, 63
Not Your Mother's Pot Roasted Chicken or Beef, 62
Southwestern Soup with Tortilla Chips, 38
Thai Coconut Noodle Soup, 36
Wild Rice and Turkey or Chicken Salad, 50

Chili
Chunky Red Chili, 32
Green Tomatillo Chili, 34

Cole slaw
Peanut Cole Slaw, 57

Cookies
Basic Chocolate Chip Cookies, 116
Chocolate Pecan Cookies, 121

Easy Sesame Almond Cookies, 116
Hazelnut Bars, 113
Lane's Bakery Nutty Crunchy Bars, 115
Mexican Wedding Cakes, 118
Peanut Butter Cookies, 117
Poppy Seed Cookies, 120

Corn
Corn Bread, 103
Grilled Corn on the Cob, 96

Cucumbers
Ginger Cukes, 56
Sweet and Sour Cucumbers with Fresh Dill, 56

Dessert
Chocolate Nut Pie, 130
Peach Crisp, 129

Dip
Guacamole, 20
Hummus, 23
Peanut Sauce, 25
Spicy Roasted Red Pepper Dip, 16
Sweet Chili Dipping Sauce, 71
Tapenade ONE, 15
Tapenade TWO, 15
Tomatillo Guacamole, 20

Dressing
Antipasto Dressing, 22
Basic Vinaigrette Dressing, 43
Citrus Dressing, 46
Cucumber Dressing, 47
Wild Rice Dressing, 51

Eggplant
Ratatouille, 88

Eggs
Heather's Favorite German-Style Oven Pancake, 107
Molly's Veggie Frittata, 87

Fish
Easy Baked Fish, 77
Super Fast Mediterranean Fish, 78
Sweet-Spicy Glazed Salmon, 78
When It Has to Be Fried Fish, 79

Frittata
Molly's Veggie Frittata, 87

Ginger
Ginger Rice Noodle Bowl , 83

Guacamole
Guacamole, 20
Tomatillo Guacamole, 20

Hummus
Hummus, 23

Leek
Pear and Leek Soup, 30
Frizzled Leek Salad, 58

Lemon
Lemon Chicken with Ripe and Green Olives, 63

Lettuce
Beef Wrapped in Lettuce, 69
Ground Turkey Wrapped in Lettuce, 70

Muffin
Carrot Muffins, 108
Gus' Blueberry Muffins, 109

Nuts
Chocolate Covered Hazelnuts, 132
Toasted Nuts, 21

Olive
Tapenade ONE, 15
Lemon Chicken with Ripe and Green Olives, 63
Tapenade TWO, 15

Pancake
Heather's Favorite German –Style Oven Pancake, 107

Pasta
Chicken Pasta Dinner, 65
Gourmet Veggie Pasta, 89
Spinach Pesto for Pasta, 90

Pear
Pear and Leek Soup, 30

Pesto
Pesto Sauce for Fish or Chicken, 81
Spinach Pesto for Pasta, 90

Polenta
Josh's Polenta with Roasted
    Vegetables, 106
Stirred Polenta, 105

Pork
Apple Braised Pork Chops, 75
Maple Chili Roasted Pork, 72
The Very Best Slow Oven Roasted Pork, 72
Tomato Curry Pork Chops, 74

Potato
Oven Fries, 93
Roasted Potato Salad, 49

Pudding
Best Chocolate Pudding, 122
Coconut Banana Custard, 123

Red Pepper
Roasted Tomato and Grilled Red Pepper
    Salad, 54
Shrimp with Excellent Almond Pepper Sauce, 80
Spicy Roasted Red Pepper Dip, 16
Tapenade TWO, 15

Rice
Fried Rice with Fruits and Vegetables, 91
Spinach Rice, 81

Rice Noodle
Ginger Rice Noodle Bowl, 83
Rice Noodle Bowl with Red Sauce, 82
Thai Coconut Noodle Soup, 36

Salad
Carrot and Pineapple Salad, 53
Carrot Salad with Lime and Cilantro, 53
Carrot Walnut Salad, 52
Chef's Salad, 44
Curried Chicken or Turkey Salad, 48
Curried Shrimp and Quinoa or Spinach
    Salad, 45

Frizzled Leek Salad, 58
Orange Carrot Salad, 52
Roasted Potato Salad, 50
Roasted Tomato and Grilled Red Pepper
    Salad, 54

Taco Salad, 44
Wild Rice and Turkey or Chicken Salad, 50

Salad Dressing
Basic Vinaigrette Dressing, 43
Citrus Dressing, 46
Cucumber Dressing, 47
Roasted Potato Salad Dressing, 49
Wild Rice Dressing, 51

Salsa
Emergency Salsa, 18
Gregg's Salsa, 17
Mango or Peach Cucumber Salsa one, 19
Mango or Peach Salsa two, 19

Sauce
Peanut Sauce, 25
Pesto Sauce for Fish or Chicken, 81
Spring Rolls Sauce, 26
Sweet Chile Dipping Sauce, 71

Seafood
Curried Shrimp and Quinoa
    or Spinach Salad, 45
Seafood Chowder, 39
Seafood Tomato Soup, 36
Shrimp with Excellent Almond Pepper
    Sauce, 80

Sorbet
Lemon Ice, 125
Strawberry or Raspberry Sorbet, 124

Soup
Basic Vegetable Beef, 38
Basic Vegetable Soup Plus, 38
Carrot Curry Soup, 29
Pear and Leek Soup, 30
Roasted Veggie Soup, 31
Seafood Chowder, 39
Seafood Tomato Soup, 36
Soup Stock, 40
Southwestern Soup with Tortilla Chips, 38
Thai Coconut Noodle Soup, 36

Spinach
Curried Shrimp and Quinoa or Spinach Salad, 45
Molly's Veggie Frittata, 87
Sautéed Spinach, 96
Spinach Rice, 81

Spring Roll
Spring Rolls Shrimp Filling, 26
Spring Rolls with Vegetable Filling, 24

Squash
Faux Hash Browns, 93
Ratatouille, 88

Stock
Soup Stock, 40

Sweet Potato
Rosemary Baked Sweet Potatoes, 94
Sort of Sweet Baked Sweet Potatoes, 95

Tomatillo
Chicken Enchiladas with Salsa Verde, 64
Green Tomatillo Chili, 34
Tomatillo Guacamole, 20

Tomato
Antipasto, 22
Roasted Tomato and Grilled Red Pepper Salad, 54
Seafood Tomato Soup, 36

Turkey
Curried Chicken or Turkey Salad, 48
Ground Turkey Wrapped in Lettuce, 70
Turkey and Pear Sauté, 67
Turkey Barbeque, 61
Wild Rice and Turkey or Chicken Salad, 50

IFC Tips

Roasting red peppers, 16
Picking a peanut butter, 29
Cleaning leeks, 30
Cooking with canned tomatoes, 31
Meet the tomatillo, 35
Coconut milk: a little goes a long way, 36
What is fish sauce?, 37
Make your own dressings, 42
Become a pepper snob, 43
Cooking your own shrimp worth the effort, 46
Try versatile quinoa, 47
What is jicama?, 48
Leftover wild rice comes in handy, 51
Try saffron for a unique flavor, 63
Tolerating aged Parmesan cheese, 67
What is Bavarian sauerkraut?, 73
No wok around?, 83
Know your milk substitutes, 103
The long and short of shortening, 113